Al

Starting and running a small business requires a great idea and a lot of hard work. Creating and marketing your unique product or service takes a lot of time, energy, and focus. With your singular focus on your outstanding product or service, you often neglect some of the necessary legalities of your business.

As a small business owner, I understand those challenges. That is why I help entrepreneurs proactively protect their small businesses through annual reviews of their business operations, affordable access to legal advice and counsel, and advocacy if faced with legal challenges so you can minimize liabilities and maximize your profits.

The first step in knowing the legal health of your business is a thorough review of your business operations. As a reader of this book, I invite you to schedule a complimentary 30 minute in-person, or Zoom, meeting with me to go over our Small Business Legal Assessment. I look forward to learning about your small business!

Schedule your free meeting today at:

LegalAdvocacyHeadquarters.com/letsmeet

Password: LAHQLetsMeet

THE TOP 10 LEGAL MISTAKES ENTREPRENEURS MAKE IN THEIR SMALL BUSINESSES

Martin Parsons

TOP 10 LEGAL MISTAKES ENTREPRENEURS
MAKE IN THEIR SMALL BUSINESSES

Published by MAEVAK Publishing

Copyright © 2022 by Martin Parsons

All rights reserved. Without limiting the rights under copyright reserved above, no part of this book may be reproduced, stored, or introduced into a retrieval system, or transmitted, in any form or by any means (electronic, mechanical, photocopying, recording, or otherwise), without the prior written permission of both the copyright owner and the publisher, except for the inclusion of brief quotations in a review.

ISBN: 978-8-9857266-0-2

For information about this title or to order other books and/or electronic media, contact the publisher:

Maevak Publishing is a small publisher that guides authors through the publishing process to help them realize their goal of getting their story or knowledge into the world. We work with a limited number of motivated authors each year to provide coaching, editing, and printing services for their books. To learn more, contact us at:

info@maevakpublishing.com

Writing a book, even a short book like this one, takes a lot of time and would not have been possible without the support and assistance of many people.

To my parents, Marty and Bertha; your example of entrepreneurship set me on the path of this new adventure. Thank you for your love and support from your #1 son!

To one of my star students, Genie Fragale; your editorial insight was invaluable to improving the readability of the book. You have a bright future ahead!

To my friend, Tom Harness, owner of Harness Digital Marketing; your insights as a small business owner provided important feedback and helped #TurnTheLightBulbOn for me!

To my in-laws, Neil and Fran Eayrs; thank you for the time you took to read it and provide your honest feedback. Thank you for your support of our new adventure!

To my brother, Matt; your viewpoint as a general manager of multiple large restaurants, combined with your newly honed skills as a writer, provided important feedback for content and structure. I'm looking forward to seeing what this next chapter of your life holds for you!

To my stepson, Evan; our discussions while watching *The Profit* helped inspire me to start my own law practice and write this book. You are a kind and gentle old soul, and I am grateful to have you in my life!

To my wife, Akami; your encouragement to complete this book by our agreed deadline kept me on task. The time and space you gave me to do the work made it possible. Your love and support in all things give me wings. I'm excited about our new adventure together!

CONTENTS

Welcome!
Who should read this book?..1
Introduction 3

Mistake 1 – Choosing the Wrong Business Entity 7
Sole Proprietorship..9
Partnership...12
LLC 14
Corporation 16
S Corporation..17
Formation of a Legal Entity 18
Assumed Name 23

Mistake 2 – Not Having Adequate Insurance........................25
Premise Liability 27
Remedial Measures 30
Insurance 31

Mistake 3 – Failing to Protect Your IP 35
Copyright...38
Trademark 40
Patent 46
Trade Secrets...47

Mistake 4 – Using Illegal Questions on Job Applications and Interviews 51

Mistake 5 – Not Having Well-Written Agreements 61
Employees 63
Suppliers/Vendors 65
Customers..68

Mistake 6 – Not Having an Employee Handbook **71**

Mistake 7 – Improperly Classifying Employees as
Independent Contractors **81**
    IRS 20-Factor Test 84
    Dangers of Misclassifying Employees as ICs 87

Mistake 8 – Improperly Paying Employees **89**
    Not Paying Workers 91
    Minimum Wage 93
    Overtime Pay 94
    Withholding and Paying Taxes 96
    Exempt Employees 96

Mistake 9 – Not Properly Counseling and Terminating
Employees **101**
    Performance Improvement Plans 103
    Terminating Employees 107

Mistake 10 – Discrimination in Employment **113**
    Federal Laws 117
    State Laws 119
    Prevention 120

Make It Happen – How I Help Entrepreneurs Proactively
Protect Their Small Businesses **123**
    The Next Step 127
    About Martin Parsons 130
    Resources 131

WHO SHOULD READ THIS BOOK?

"The critical ingredient is getting off your butt and doing something. It's as simple as that. A lot of people have ideas, but there are few who decide to do something about them now. Not tomorrow. Not next week. But today. The true entrepreneur is a doer, not a dreamer." Nolan Bushnell, founder of Atari.

If you are an entrepreneur with the dream of starting your own business, or have already started your own business, and haven't had the time or patience to learn about some of the important legal issues that can come up in your business, this short book is for you.

Starting and running a business is hard but rewarding work. It takes a lot of time and energy, but the freedom that comes from being your own boss outweighs the work and sacrifices - most of the time. If concerns about legal issues creep into your mind at times or keep you up at night, this book is for you.

This book discusses ten common legal mistakes entrepreneurs make when setting up their business and in the ongoing operations of their business. This is by no means an exhaustive list of mistakes we can make in running our businesses or an in-depth discussion of them.

I tried not to use too much legal language, but some of these concepts just require it. For that, I apologize in advance. In each chapter, I provide additional information and resources for further exploration. At the end of the book, I provide the website where you can access those resources. I also provide an opportunity for a free meeting with me to conduct a legal risk assessment of your business.

The legal challenges of a small business owner are as varied as the types of businesses we own. Yet there are also many common problems we all face and can avoid. This book will help you identify those common legal problems in your business and offer solutions to avoid them.

INTRODUCTION

"There's no shortage of remarkable ideas, what's missing is the will to execute them." Seth Godin; author and entrepreneur.

"Success is not final; failure is not fatal: it is the courage to continue that counts." Winston Churchill.

In the summer of 1993, I purchased a bar and live music venue with a close friend of mine. I had managed a bar at a private country club and a happening hotel nightclub in a Big 10 college town in the Midwest. He was a video DJ with the music connections to book the entertainment. At that point in my career, I thought I knew enough to dive headfirst into this partnership without any mentoring or legal advice. Four months later, with strong pressure from his father who had loaned us most of the startup funds, my partner, and friend, forced me out of the business through a buyout. It was a valuable learning experience as well as the kick in the pants I needed to get out of the bar business.

Several lifetimes later and after serving 26 years in the military and attending law school, I am now an attorney, and small business owner, with a passion for helping entrepreneurs proactively protect their small businesses through affordable access to legal advice and counsel, so small business owners can minimize liabilities and maximize profits.

The chapters are in somewhat of the order of the steps you would go through in setting up your business. Not exactly, because it isn't necessarily a linear journey. So, you can start from the beginning and follow the Legal Mistakes Roadmap or skip to the chapter that discusses the specific legal issue you want to learn about.

As a lawyer, I must give the disclaimer that this is not intended as legal advice, nor does it create an attorney-client relationship. This is for educational and informational purposes with the intent of helping you see potential legal pitfalls, suggesting possible solutions, and providing resources to get more information. I am licensed to practice law in Illinois and Missouri, so the beginning information in each chapter is generic and references "some states" or "your state." Then, I typically follow with Illinois-specific information. I encourage you to consult an attorney for advice related to your specific state and situation.

This is also not a solicitation for your business. As an attorney, I am bound by our ethical rules of non-solicitation. While the rules prohibit solicitation if it involves coercion, duress, or harassment, and since this is a one-sided conversation and you cannot express any desire not to be solicited,

I will err on the side of caution and provide this blanket disclaimer.

With the legal stuff out of the way, let's talk about one of the first mistakes entrepreneurs make when starting their businesses – **choosing the wrong legal business entity.**

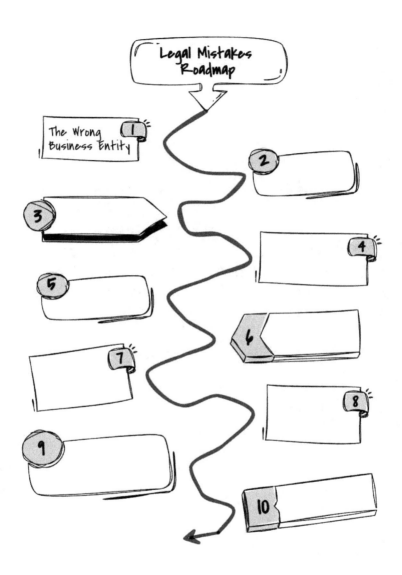

"Organizing is what you do before you do something. So that when you do it, it is not all mixed up." A.A. Milne; Author, *Winnie-the-Pooh*.

MISTAKE 1

CHOOSING THE WRONG LEGAL BUSINESS ENTITY

One of the most important initial decisions an entrepreneur makes when planning and starting their business is the selection of their legal business entity. The proper selection of a business entity impacts your business and individual income, minimizes tax consequences, and determines the level of legal protection you have from unforeseen financial or legal problems. The most common business entities are sole proprietorship, partnership, limited liability company, S Corporation, and Corporation.

Sole Proprietorship

A sole proprietorship is the most basic business structure. It is a business owned and operated by an individual who is the sole owner. One individual owns and operates the business. Sole proprietors do not have any legal identity other than the business they're operating. They generally must be a "real" person. Many small businesses start as sole proprietorships. Often, the entrepreneur starts the business and names it after themselves, e.g., Smith Lawncare; Williams Plumbing & Heating; or Garcia Electrical. Other owners name their business to describe their product or service, or create a brand, and don't use their own names, e.g., Best Darn BBQ; Paisley Productions; or Get Fit Gym.

In Illinois, if you choose to conduct business as a sole proprietor and do not use your real name, you must register the name of the business as an assumed name with the County Clerk of the county where your primary business office is located. You must provide your full name and address of the primary location of the business and any other locations where you conduct business. After filing with the County Clerk, you must place a notice in a newspaper of general circulation published within the county in which the certificate is filed for three consecutive weeks. The first publication must be within 15 days of filing the certificate with the County Clerk. Proof of publication must be provided to the County Clerk within 50 days from the date of filing the certificate. Once the clerk receives the proof of publication, they will give you a receipt as proof of filing. If you change the name of the business or the address of the business, you must notify the clerk of the change. If you form your business as any of the remaining entities discussed below, you do not need to file the assumed name with the county. *See* 805 ILCS 405, Assumed Business Name Act.

A sole proprietorship is best suited for a simple business with low risk including part-time businesses, direct sellers, contractors, consultants, or new start-ups when the owner wants to test their ideas before creating a more formal business structure. If the business is sued, the owner is personally liable for all costs and judgments against the business. An adverse judgment against a sole proprietor could force the owner into personal bankruptcy.

As the owner, the sole proprietor is personally liable for all the business's debts, tax liabilities, and other obligations. When a sole proprietorship fails, the assets and liabilities are transferred to the owner. Even without adverse legal actions, a failed business could force a sole proprietor into personal bankruptcy.

Tax filing for the sole proprietorship is easier than other forms of business classification. The owner simply includes the profit or loss from the business on their personal tax return using the IRS Form 1040. Since the sole proprietor works for themselves, self-employment taxes will be included in any amount that may be owed to the government.

If you are currently operating as a sole proprietorship or considering beginning your business as one, think about the potential liabilities your business could incur. Make a list of worst-case scenarios that could happen to your business and try to give them a monetary value. Once you have that total amount, you can better determine whether you should continue as a sole proprietorship. You can also use that value to make sure you have adequate insurance to help mitigate the risks you have as a sole proprietor.

Partnership

A partnership is a business owned by two or more individuals. It is a corporate form of business ownership that is created by two or more business partners who agree to invest financially in the business and share in the profits or losses. However, the partners are also each entitled to personal tax benefits. For example, the partners share profits and losses and can elect to deduct any losses from their personal taxes.

The partnership has a legally separate identity from the individual owners. The partners are responsible for the business's liabilities and debts and are required to file a partnership tax return. A partnership, like a sole proprietorship, must be a "real" person. When a partnership is closed, the assets and liabilities are transferred to the partners.

There are two types of partnership, the general partnership, and the limited partnership. In a general partnership, the partners share equally in the commitments and responsibilities of the business. This could become a problem if one of the partners enters into a bad agreement or makes some other significant mistake. All partners are responsible for the liabilities that may come from these mistakes.

Partners can also be sued individually by third parties. If a general partnership has financial difficulties, then the partners may have to utilize their personal assets to cover the shortfall or let the partnership fail.

A limited partnership, as the name implies, has limitations on the partners' liabilities for financial difficulties and lawsuits. In most states, a limited partnership must be registered with the Secretary of State, which involves fees to the state and more strict record-keeping to maintain the formality of the limited partnership.

While a written agreement setting out the rights and obligations of each partner is helpful to the running of the partnership, in most states, a written agreement between the parties is not required. The association of two or more persons to carry on as co-owners of a business for profit could form a partnership, even if they did not intend to form a partnership. The best way to create a legal partnership is to file the required paperwork with the Secretary of State and draft a partnership agreement. A partnership agreement is important because it sets out each partner's rights, roles, and responsibilities. It should include sections to discuss how new partners can be added, how partners leave, and how the partnership can be terminated. The agreement should be drafted with a vision of the future, both for growth, and demise. Try to think of all the ways the partnership could go wrong and how you want to address them if it happens.

In Illinois, partnerships are governed by the Uniform Partnership Act, 805 ILCS 206, and the Limited Liability Partnership Act, 805 ILCS 215. Illinois has two forms of partnerships, Limited Partnerships, and Limited Liability Partnerships. In Illinois, you cannot form a partnership online, you must file paper forms. The Secretary of State's website provides the downloadable forms, costs, and filing instructions.

Limited Liability Company

A limited liability company (LLC) is a business organization that provides legal and financial protections to its owners and managers. Owners of an LLC are called "members" and the organization is called a "company." As the name implies, each member of the LLC has limited liability.

The structure of an LLC makes it more flexible than the other types of legal business entities. The level of involvement by the members, as well as the share of profits and losses, can be determined in any manner agreed upon by the members and included in the LLC operating agreement. The LLC operating agreement is the written document that provides the rules for how the LLC will conduct its corporate business, including governance, rights and obligations of members, how meetings of members are conducted, the members' capital contributions, allocation of profits and losses among the members, how membership is transferred or terminated, how the LLC is dissolved and terminated, and other miscellaneous provisions. The LLC operating agreement is not typically required to be filed with the Secretary of State.

Companies formed as LLCs are "pass-through" entities, where profits are passed on to owners and taxed as personal income instead of corporate income. This avoids the double taxation that occurs with a corporation's profits. To best understand the tax implications of your specific business, I encourage you to seek advice from a certified public accountant (CPA).

For tax purposes, an LLC has a Federal Employer Identification Number (EIN) also known as a Federal Tax Identification Number issued by the IRS. Even if you don't have employees, an LLC must have an EIN. You can apply for an EIN for free from the IRS. Beware of websites that offer to assist you with obtaining your EIN but charge a fee. There is *no* fee to apply for an EIN when completing the application online from the IRS website listed below.

https://www.irs.gov/businesses/small-businesses-self-employed/apply-for-an-employer-identification-number-ein-online

Corporation

A corporation is a business entity formed to make a profit. Why else would you spend all the time and money to form a corporation if it wasn't to make a profit? (Yes, you could form a non-profit corporation, but even though the owners don't personally profit from the enterprise, the organization is still run to generate revenue and profit so it can deliver the services it was formed to provide.) It is run by a board of directors who are elected by the shareholders. A corporation is considered a separate legal entity from its owners, who are called shareholders and can own property, sue, and be sued in a contract. It provides liability protection for its owners' personal assets.

Corporations are subject to double taxation. The net income to the business is taxed before the profits are distributed to the shareholders. Then the shareholders must pay taxes on their dividends from the corporation. This can be avoided by electing to be taxed as an S corporation.

When my friend and I bought the bar together I mentioned in the introduction, we chose to form a corporation. As bar owners, I knew we needed to protect our personal assets in case of a lawsuit, even though we didn't have any personal assets at the time. We had high hopes of great success and prosperity! However, we didn't create any bylaws that would have governed how our business relationship would be set up and the work divided between us or how it would terminate if the relationship went bad. The bylaws would have given me some protection, or at least some options and due process, against being forced out by my business partner. An important lesson in creating and observing corporate formalities.

S Corporation

An S corporation is a business corporation that allows the shareholders to deduct the business's operating expenses from their personal tax return. The shareholders have made an election to be taxed under subchapter S rather than subchapter C, which is the normal corporate tax section. The shareholders are responsible for paying the tax on the income the company earns. An S corporation is like a sole proprietorship for tax purposes, which means it will report its income and expenses from the corporation on the individual shareholder's tax return. This allows the shareholders to avoid double taxation by paying corporate tax, as well as the individual income tax on profits, and possibly the payroll tax on the corporate owner's income.

After forming the corporation, if you choose to make a subchapter S election, you must obtain and complete Form 2553 from the IRS. Since an S corporation is primarily a tax structure, I recommend talking to a certified public accountant to make sure you file the proper paperwork and follow the required formalities.

Formation of a Legal Entity

Now that we have an overview of several legal business entities, let's discuss generally how to formally create them in your state. The formation of legal business entities is governed by state law. Every state has different rules, forms, and processes (and costs) for forming a business entity. The starting point for properly forming a legal business entity is usually with your Secretary of State.

Most states allow the formation of legal entities entirely online. This helps you quickly obtain legal status for your business and begin selling your product or providing the service of your business. However, before attempting to register your business, you must conduct a search of the Secretary of State's corporate listings for entities with the same or similar name. You should conduct this search ***before*** registering a domain name for the business or buying business cards and stationery. The Secretary of State will not register your business if it has the same or similar name as one already in use by another business. The name must be distinguishable from any other name already registered with the Secretary. I also suggest doing an internet search to see if anyone else in the country is using your business name. This may not be a concern if you have no interest in conducting business outside your state and no intention of trademarking the name or logo, which I will cover in **Mistake 3 – Failing to Protect Your Intellectual Property**. Once you have determined your corporate name is not in use, you can proceed to register your corporate entity.

If you choose to form an LLC or corporation, you will need to name a registered agent. The registered agent is someone who can accept service for any lawsuits that may be filed against the legal entity. In most states, you can name yourself as the registered agent, if you reside in the state where you are forming the legal entity. If you are forming in another state where you do not live, you need to name an agent who lives in that state. Many organizations provide registered agent services. Some attorneys offer this service to their business clients as a benefit of working with them or as a package when managing your corporate books. Having your business attorney as your registered agent provides several benefits. They will receive any service of process should you ever be sued, rather than having the sheriff show up at your place of business during business hours when customers might be there. Regardless of who may be at fault, it is not the best impression for your business. It provides peace of mind that you won't miss a court deadline because you were out of the office, or it got buried in a stack of mail. A registered agent can also help keep up with the regular state renewal filings and corporate documents.

As part of helping you proactively protect your business, we provide registered agent services for our Illinois clients. To learn more about our services visit our website:

LegalAdvocacyHeadquarters.com

In Illinois, you register your LLC by filing Articles of Organization online or hard copy by mail to the Secretary of State. If you are going to file online, I suggest printing out the paper form to use to gather the necessary information before starting the online application.

If you are incorporating as an LLC, most states require the inclusion of "Limited Liability Company," "L.L.C.," or "LLC" in the name of the entity. It is typically tacked on at the end of the name. For example, "Legal Advocacy Headquarters, LLC." You can incorporate as a single-member LLC in most states, which doesn't require the names of any more members than yourself. You will need to create a purpose statement for your LLC and provide it to the state on your application. Each state has a preferred format.

Even though you aren't required to provide it in all states, you should draft an Operating Agreement (OA) for your LLC. The OA outlines your business's financial and functional decisions including rules, regulations, and provisions. This can be as simple or complicated as necessary depending on how many members you have and the value of your business. An OA is important because it protects the members from personal liability by maintaining the corporate formalities. Without an OA, your LLC could look like a sole proprietorship or partnership. At a minimum, the OA should include the percentage of each member's ownership; voting rights and responsibilities; powers and duties of members; distribution of profits and losses; method of holding meetings; buyout and buy-sell rules and the procedures for transferring interest or in the event of death of a member.

Like the Partnership Agreement, you should plan for the growth of your company, and for what happens if it fails, or you choose to terminate it. If you have more than one member, what happens if that association goes bad? Include language that explains how the member can withdraw, or how they can be involuntarily removed. If the leaving member has a capital contribution, determine how their share will be calculated and paid.

The OA should be signed and kept with the other important corporate and business documents. If you have contracted for registered agent service, the agent will often safeguard these documents as part of their service.

If you are forming a corporation, most states require the inclusion of "Corporation," "Company," "Incorporated," "Limited" or an abbreviation of one of those. For example, "Legal Advocacy Headquarters, Corporation" or "Legal Advocacy Headquarters, Inc." As with the LLC, you will need to provide a purpose statement on your Articles of Incorporation to the state. You need to list the types of shares, number of shares authorized, number of shares to be issued, and the price of the shares. You may need to list any restrictions on the share types. The number of directors and their names and addresses must be included as well. Most states require the reporting of the estimated value of the property the corporation will own and an estimate of the gross amount of business that will be transacted in its first year.

Like an LLC's Operating Agreement, a corporation's bylaws govern the way the corporation does its business. It discusses the corporation's purposes, the issuance of shares, the makeup of the board of directors, how officers are named and compensated, meetings of the board of directors and shareholders, how dividends are paid, and how shares are transferred. Like the other agreements discussed, plan for growth and the end. Try and think of all the ways things could go wrong and include language to address it. You won't think of everything, but a well-thought-out agreement should cover most of the likely scenarios.

As you can see, even from this brief description of the corporate formation process, forming a corporation is more complicated than forming an LLC. Additionally, there are ongoing, regular corporate meetings and reporting formalities that add time and expense to this form of business entity.

For Illinois residents, the Illinois Secretary of State website has many resources to further assist you in picking your business entity and to guide you in applying to the state.

Assumed Name or DBA

A lesser-known "trick" to remove the "Limited Liability Company," "L.L.C.", "LLC," "Corporation," "Company," "Incorporated," or "Limited" identifier from your business name that you use daily is to file an "Assumed Name" or "Doing Business As" registration with your state. If you do not do this, you must include the LLC or corporate identifiers after your name on everything you do as a business, including signs, business cards, letterhead, and advertising. It cleans up the name of your business and makes it easier to brand. For example,

"Legal Advocacy Headquarters, LLC" becomes "Legal Advocacy Headquarters."

Also, you can have multiple companies under one umbrella LLC or corporation by using assumed names. For example, "Legal Advocacy Headquarters, LLC" could do business under the assumed names, "Legal Advocacy Headquarters," "Legal Advocacy HQ," and "Paisley Productions."

In Illinois, an LLC Assumed Name adoption is good for five years and costs $150, or an initially reduced amount depending on what year you register in the five-year cycle. A Corporate Assumed Name adoption costs $150 to register. This can also be done online through the Secretary of State's website.

Now that you have information to help you choose the correct legal entity, the next mistake entrepreneurs often make is **not having adequate insurance**.

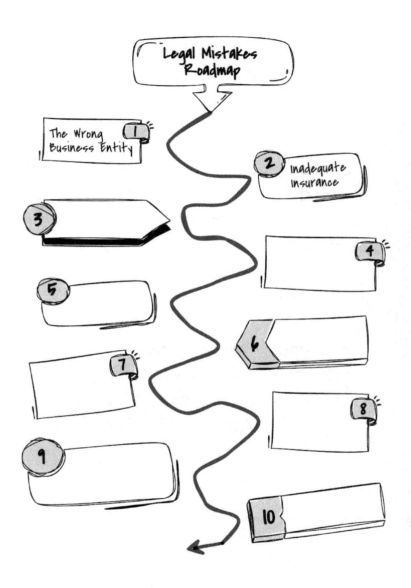

"Every business and every product have risks. You can't get around it." Lee Iacocca; American automotive executive.

"If you don't invest in risk management, it doesn't matter what business you're in, it's a risky business." Gary Cohn; American business leader.

MISTAKE 2

NOT HAVING ADEQUATE INSURANCE

As an attorney, I see liabilities everywhere! When you open your doors for business, you take a risk that customers and other visitors may be injured or cause property damage. Your small business has the potential to incur liabilities on and off your premises. You have a responsibility to them to ensure your premises are fit for their intended purpose and safe. You owe it to your business, from a financial standpoint, to minimize the risks and to insure against them.

This chapter will look at some forms of premises liability for businesses. I'll discuss some best practices for minimizing your exposure to these risks. Finally, we'll look at the types of insurance that can help protect your business and its assets against these liabilities.

Premises Liability

Premises liability arises when someone is injured from an incident when you knew or should have known of a dangerous situation and did not take steps to prevent harm to them. Your premises include its site, structures (buildings, walls, fences, roads), and utilities (water, gas, electricity). If someone is injured on your premises, they may have a right to bring legal action against you. That includes liabilities incurred by employees, customers, or others who come into your physical location.

Some common examples of premises liability are slip and fall accidents, snow and ice accidents, defective conditions, negligent or inadequate security leading to injury or assault, and inadequate maintenance of the premises.

Most states have adopted premises liability laws making a business owner responsible for its business operations, the acts of its employees, and the condition of the property. By law, a business owner owes a duty to maintain the premises in a manner that is safe for the public. This includes maintaining the premises without defects, as well as ensuring that the premises are prepared for entry by the public. You can, for instance, fail to warn of unsafe conditions that your employees regularly use, such as stairs, holes, or uneven ground. If a visitor is harmed because of these conditions, they may be able to bring a claim against your business.

Liability to the public generally arises when a business owner allows a third party to use its premises and then the third party is injured. For example, a restaurant owner owes a duty to a public patron to maintain the premises in a safe condition, and that includes sidewalks, driveways, and parking lots, as well as the restaurant itself. If a patron slips and falls, the restaurant owner may be liable for the damages, if the patron can show that the sidewalk was not in good condition and the owner knew, or should have known, about the problem and didn't repair it.

Legal responsibility for injuries incurred on a business's premises becomes complicated when the business owner leases the property from a landlord. Each party's responsibility for the repair and maintenance of the premises should be clearly defined in the lease agreement.

The business can be liable for an injured person who is a trespasser, licensee, or business invitee. Let's define these legal terms to make them easier to understand. A trespasser is someone who enters the property without permission, like a robber. A licensee is someone who is not expressly invited but legally allowed. Like an advertising salesperson soliciting business without an appointment. An invitee is someone who is invited or expected by the property owner for a commercial or professional purpose, such as a customer of the business. Licensees and invitees are owed a duty of care, but in some states that duty may be different for each.

Premises liability is governed by several laws that vary by state. Some of these are the common-law duty of care, the negligence standard, and the products liability act. Other laws, such as the Consumer Product Safety Act and the standards set out by the Occupational Safety and Health Administration

(OSHA), impose additional duties on businesses. Additionally, there are other common forms of premises liability, such as public liability, negligence, strict liability, and intentional torts.

Remedial Measures

Business owners often worry, and rightfully so, about being held liable for injuries or damage caused by or on their property. However, there are several steps you can take to minimize your liability exposure. First, you should make sure your premises are safe for public use. One way is to conduct a thorough and regular investigation of the premises and to eliminate or reduce any defects that may lead to accidents. This means making sure that sidewalks, driveways, and parking lots are in good condition, and your business is free of defects that would cause someone to fall and injure themselves. A daily checklist is an excellent tool to remind you or your employees to complete these tasks, to confirm they were completed, and to provide support in case of litigation. At a minimum, include the name of the task, a block for the day and time the task was completed, and a block for the initials of the person who completed the task.

Promptly clean up spills or accidents and place "wet floor" signs out when appropriate. Make sure all floors are free of debris, loose flooring, and other trip hazards. Make sure your stairs are sturdy and have proper guard rails. Maintain your land/property by clearing debris after a storm, removing snow, and making sure your parking lot and walkways are free of ice. Maintain adequate building security whenever possible, including having security cameras and the ability to lock doors and fences. This will reduce the risk of causing an injury to a person who enters your property. You should document these efforts in writing and with photographs. This can help with your defense should you be sued for an incident or accident.

Another way is to warn of any hazardous conditions on the premises and to instruct employees to use caution when working on or near hazardous conditions. If a hazardous condition occurs, mark that location with a warning sign and attempt to correct it as quickly as possible. If you are unable to fix it promptly, divert employees or customers from that area until the hazard can be fixed.

Insurance

One of the first steps you should take to protect yourself against premises liability is to purchase insurance. There are different types of insurance a business can purchase to protect itself against the financial risk of being sued for premises liability. One type of insurance is a commercial general liability policy, also known as a CGL policy. A CGL policy provides coverage for any bodily injury or property damage that occurs on the premises of the business, regardless of who caused the injury or damage.

Many CGL policies include coverage for premises liability, but it is important to verify the extent of the coverage and the exclusions or limits on the coverage. If you are a sole proprietor, the exercise you did in the first chapter to determine your potential financial liability will help you and your insurance agent determine the proper amount of insurance you need. If you are operating a business out of your home, you may want to consider purchasing separate policies for your business and your home.

Liability for off-premises injuries or property damage caused by an employee of the business is also typically covered by a CGL policy. This type of coverage is intended to protect the business from being held liable for injuries and property damage caused by the employees while they are working off the premises of the business.

Another type of coverage a business owner will be required to purchase is a workers' compensation policy. Nearly every state requires a business owner to carry workers' compensation coverage. A workers' compensation policy provides coverage for any injury to an employee that occurs on the job, such as lifting heavy equipment or slipping on a wet or oily surface. It covers medical expenses and a portion of lost wages for your employees who are injured in the course of their job duties. Deciding not to carry workers' compensation insurance puts your business at great financial risk. You could be sued by an employee for workplace injuries or fined by the state for breaking the law. Workers' compensation coverage premiums are another cost of doing business that should be included in your operating budget.

I don't want to paint this as all doom and gloom for the business owner. Even if a person is injured on your premises, most states look at the comparative fault of the person who is injured. The invitee or licensee must use reasonable care to keep themselves safe on your premises. In pure comparative negligence states, if they don't use reasonable care, any recovery in a lawsuit can be reduced by their percentage of fault. In modified comparative negligence states, if they are found to be 50% - 51% at fault or more, depending on the state, the injured party cannot recover any compensation. Illinois is a modified comparative negligence state. An injured party may recover damages only if they are less than 50% at fault for the injury or damages. *See* 735 ICLS 5/2-1116.

General and premises liability in a business can be complicated. However, even the most careful and attentive business owner cannot prevent every injury or all damage to its property. You should consult with a knowledgeable insurance agent before opening your business to customers and employees. Your best preventative measure is to attempt to keep your premises free of hazards, warn of hazards you can't repair or control, and insure yourself against the possibility of a problem.

If something happens on your premises, document everything in writing, take pictures and contact your insurance carrier. Get as many witness statements as you can, as soon as you can. Accurate memories of events fade quickly. Employees should not be coerced or enticed to provide witness statements.

In your interactions with the injured person, show care and compassion toward them, however, don't discuss whether you knew or should have known about the premises defect. Instruct your employees who may interact with this person to do the same. Let the insurance company and their lawyers deal with the fault and liability.

Now that I've opened your eyes to the world of premises liability, let's look at another mistake entrepreneurs make – **failing to protect your intellectual property.**

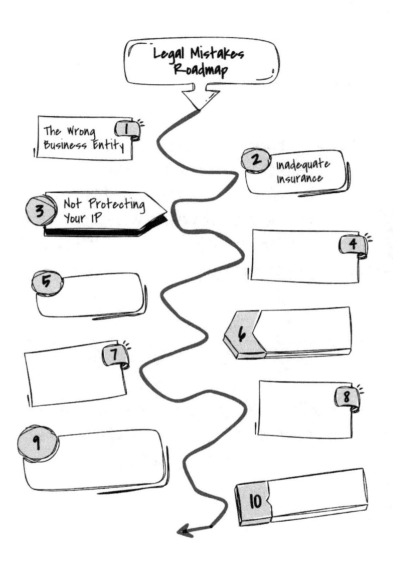

"Intellectual property is playing an increasingly important role for our group. It's just a fact of life in our business now that you have to cultivate and protect IP." Rudy Provoost; Belgian entrepreneur.

"Intellectual property has the shelf life of a banana." Bill Gates; Co-founder of Microsoft.

MISTAKE 3

FAILING TO PROTECT YOUR INTELLECTUAL PROPERTY

Every small business has some form of intellectual property. From its name to its logo to the copy in its advertisements. Failing to protect that intellectual property can dilute your brand identity and cost you money. Your protected intellectual property also adds value to your business should you decide to sell it in the future.

Intellectual property, or IP, are concepts or ideas that are protected by law, such as copyright, trademark, patent, and trade secrets. IP is a form of ownership that gives its owner the right to profit from their ideas. In a business context, the law protects the use of logos, names, and characters of companies, inventions, designs, brands, and ideas, to name a few.

Your new ideas, if unprotected, are easy prey for unscrupulous actors. It's important to know how to protect your intellectual property rights.

There are four categories of intellectual property: copyrights, trademarks, patents, and trade secrets.

Intellectual property can be classified into four types: copyrights, trademarks, patents, and trade secrets. These four types of intellectual property protect the value of your ideas and creations. Copyrights cover the content and any creativity of a work (book, song, etc.) for 70 years after the death of the author. Trademarks can protect a brand name or logo for unlimited years if proper renewal procedures are followed. Patents protect an invention for 20 years. Trade secrets protect facts, ideas, designs, techniques, processes, software, blueprints, patterns, methods, and business information.

Copyright

Copyright is a legal right that gives a person or company exclusive ownership of creative work. It is a form of protection granted to the authors of original works, including literary, dramatic, musical, artistic, and certain other intellectual works. It is a legal right that allows creators to control how their work is used. The creator of the work is also known as the copyright holder.

Copyright law gives an author, or the right holder, the exclusive right to make or authorize copies of a work, to publish the work, or other exclusive rights. Copyright grants an author or owner exclusive rights to reproduce, distribute, perform, display, and create derivative works based on the original work.

The owner of the copyright has the right to prevent someone else from making an unauthorized copy of the work. Copyright generally continues for the life of the author plus 70 years, subject to statutory or court-imposed extensions.

As soon as an idea is written down, the author of that idea is entitled to enforce their rights against others who may attempt to duplicate it or claim it as their own. You can use the © symbol along with your name and the year of publication as soon as you publish the work. Official registration with the U.S. Copyright Office is not required before using the symbol. However, the proper filing of a copyright with the U.S. Copyright Office serves as *prima facie*, or sufficient, evidence of ownership of the idea and enables the copyright holder to sue the infringing user for damages and attorney's fees.

The U.S. Copyright Office handles all official registrations in the United States. At the time of publication of this book, the registration fees start at $45 for a single author/same claimant application filed online.

Generally, copyright ownership can be proven through an examination of the author's official records and registration with the Copyright Office. For more information on copyright registration and transfer, see the Copyright Office's helpful resources.

https://www.copyright.gov/

Trademark

A registered trademark is a legal right to the exclusive use of a word, phrase, symbol, design, or a distinctive combination of letters, or other design or symbol used by a business to identify its goods or services and distinguish them from other businesses. It is a form of intellectual property that protects the goodwill that a trademark creates in the minds of consumers. It is an important component of your brand.

It helps consumers distinguish products or services as belonging to one company instead of another. Think of the McDonald's golden arches, Apple's iPod, or Nike's swoosh.

Even without registering, you become a trademark owner when you start using your trademark with your goods or services. However, those rights are limited and only apply to the geographic area where you provide your goods or services. A trademark registered with the U.S. Patent and Trademark Office, (USPTO) provides broader, nationwide rights and protections. With a registered trademark, every time you use the trademark you can use the TM (Trademark), SM (Servicemark), or ® symbol with it.

As business owners, one of the first things we do after registering our business with the state, and sometimes even before that, is to secure the domain name for our business. However, registration of your domain name alone does not provide any trademark rights. Without proper trademark research and registration, you could be required to surrender a domain name if it infringes on another business owner's trademark rights. This could cost your business money in legal fees as well as lost goodwill and brand recognition.

Trademark search and registration is a service we provide to help you proactively protect your business. For more information visit our website:

LegalAdvocacyHeadquarters.com

The use and registration of a business name with your state does not give you trademark rights either. Another business, that later successfully trademarks your business name, could try, and keep you from using your business name if they believe that consumers could confuse their business with yours. The standard the USPTO uses is "likelihood of confusion."

To move from the negative consequences of not trademarking your name or logo to something more positive - there is monetary value in protecting them. If you decide to sell your business in the future, the value of the business is made up of several factors. One of those factors is the protected name and logo of your business. If you have built a good name for your business and have strong brand awareness that you have legally protected, the value of that brand can be included as a line item on the calculation of value in a buy-sell agreement. Conversely, no prospective buyer wants to risk their investment in a business that has built a strong name, reputation, and brand in its field if they are not protected.

Applying for trademark protection can be done entirely online. At the time of publication of this book, the application fee is $250 for each class of goods/services using the Trademark Electronic Application System (TEAS) Plus online filing system. The USPTO application fee is nonrefundable. So, filing an accurate application for a distinct mark is important.

Before applying to register your trademark, you must thoroughly research the USPTO filings, state business registrations, website domain registrations, and the internet, in general, to determine whether there are any already existing similar business names or logos. Without conducting that search, you don't know if there are any similar marks already registered or in the application process. If there are, your application will be quickly denied, and you will lose the application fee. You would then need to decide on a new name or logo and start the process over again. This could be a significant problem if you have already been using the name and people in your area know you and your business by that name.

For most businesses that have a name and logo, you need to decide if you should file more than one application to protect your brand. If the name of your business is unique and significant and is contained in the logo, you might consider filing a standard character mark application for the name alone. This provides the broadest protection for your name. But if you have a distinctive logo that does not contain the business name, you may want to apply for a stylized mark for the logo as well. The cost to file doubles when filing two different types of applications. The opportunity for error also increases, especially when applying for the stylized mark for the logo.

It's important to select the correct class of goods for your product or service. If you choose incorrectly your application will be denied with a loss of application fees. Some marks require applying for several classes of goods/services to secure the most protection. For example, a service business such as a restaurant will file under 043 for its name and logo. But if that restaurant is going to sell merchandise like hats or t-shirts, it will also need to file under 025. This application would cost $500 because there are two classes of goods. If you file two different applications, as we discussed in the preceding paragraph, the fee will double to $1000 because you filed two different application types for two classes of goods.

The application will ask your "basis" for filing. Are you currently using the name or logo now in your business or do you intend to use it in the future? If you are currently using the name or logo, you file under the "use in commerce basis" of the Trademark Act Section 1(a). If you just came up with your awesome idea for a business and are not using the name or logo yet, you will file under the "intent-to-use basis" of Section 1(b). If you are using the mark now, you will need to provide the date the mark was used anywhere on the goods or in connection with the service and the date the mark was first used in commerce. You also need to provide a specimen of the mark in use. Proper selection of the specimen is important to an easy registration without demands from the USPTO examiner for a different specimen.

After you apply, it is reviewed by an examiner at the USPTO to determine whether it meets the standard for registration and if the owner is qualified to register the mark. Any rejections of the application by the USPTO examiner are called Office Actions. They explain why the mark was rejected and ask for clarification, changes, or additions. You are required to respond to all Office Actions within six months of the mailing date. If you do not respond promptly the application will be considered abandoned.

If the application is approved, the USPTO will notify you of the approval. Then you must maintain compliance with the standards for registration to keep the mark protected by the law. These standards include continued use of the mark in commerce and paying the ongoing registration fees at the determined milestones. The first milestone is between the 5th and 6th year of registration. You must file a Section 8 Affidavit to confirm you are still using the mark in commerce. With the Section 8 Affidavit, you can also submit a Section 15 Declaration of Incontestability. With this statement, the trademark owner claims incontestable rights in the trademark for five years. The filing of this statement makes the mark incontestable and various aspects of the registration cannot be challenged by third parties. Between the 9th and 10th year of registration, you must file a combined Section 8 and Section 9 filing. Then for each successive 10-year period, you must file a combined Section 8 and 9 filing to continue to maintain your rights in the mark.

Once you have a registered trademark, you can assert all the rights in the mark. This also gives you a basis for a future dispute of ownership over a trademark. As the trademark owner, you can enforce your rights against an infringer, whether from a customer, competitor, or another company in federal court.

The USPTO website has many good resources to learn more about the process and to file for trademark protection.

https://www.uspto.gov/trademarks

On its face, the application process is straightforward. However, as mentioned here, several places in the process can be tricky and if not done correctly could cost you valuable time and money. There are also important renewal forms and deadlines to keep track of after registration. Considering the important value a trademark can bring to your business, and the filing fees alone that could be lost, if not filed properly, consulting an attorney for assistance with this process, could be a worthwhile investment in your business.

Patent

A patent is a form of IP that grants an inventor, or patent holder, legal rights for a limited period. This is known as a patent or patent term. A patent, or patent term, gives an inventor exclusive rights to the invention for a limited time after the filing of the patent application, typically 20 years. It is governed by different laws than copyright and trademark. The patent is granted for a particular process, product, design, machine, or article and it may be awarded to an inventor or an applicant for a patent. It gives the inventor the right to prevent others from making, using, selling, or importing the new invention without the inventor's permission.

A patent only applies within the United States and the application must be filed with the U.S. Patent and Trademark Office (USPTO).

The application and registration process for patents is more complicated than for trademarks. A business that is centered around an invention has too much riding on the invention to consider applying for a patent without legal assistance. Without proper patent protection, that business would quickly die if its invention were stolen because it is not protected. Because of the significance of that protection, I am not spending much time discussing the application process and strongly recommend consulting an attorney for assistance with a patent application. However, if you would like to learn more about the process before consulting with an attorney, the USPTO website has several good resources.

https://www.uspto.gov/patents

Trade Secrets

Trade secrets are a crucial part of the ecosystem of business development. They are the formula, recipe, design, or manufacturing process that a company considers confidential. A trade secret can be any information a company considers confidential, but not all confidential information is a trade secret. It is often information about how a product or service is developed and sold. Trade secrets are protected from other companies and from employees who have access to this information through a variety of legal tools. Traditional trade secrets are closely tied to patents, copyrights, trademarks, and trade names. They have value to others who do not have legitimate access to this information.

To be legally protectable, trade secrets should be written down or documented electronically. The document must contain a notice of confidentiality. For example, a cover page with the following information:

CONFIDENTIAL. *This document contains trade secrets or otherwise confidential information owned by the Company. Access to and use of this information is strictly limited and controlled by the Company. This document may not be copied, distributed, or otherwise disclosed outside the Company's facilities except under appropriate precautions to maintain the confidentiality, and may not be used in any way not expressly authorized by the Company.*

Additional warnings should be applied to all pages of the documents. Such as, "Confidential Information" or "Confidential Information of the Company."

Once it is documented, the law requires that adequate protections be made to keep the trade secrets secure. Keep the electronic files in password-protected locations with strict access restrictions or secure hard copy documents in locked file cabinets or in a safe.

New employees should sign a nondisclosure agreement that sets out the limitations, scope, and enforcement options for the protection of the company's trade secrets. All departing employees should be reminded of the obligations of the nondisclosure agreement and the potential legal ramifications of violating the agreement. These agreements should be rigorously enforced by the business. If violations of the agreement are not enforced, your business could lose the ability to enforce violations in the future and more importantly, lose the value of those trade secrets in the marketplace.

If your business has trade secrets in its portfolio, you should create a policy for the creation, documentation, and protection of those secrets. If you would like to get a sample policy, I have included one in the resource material that accompanies this book.

Now that you know how to properly protect your intellectual property, let's look at the next mistake - **using illegal questions on your job applications and in interviews.**

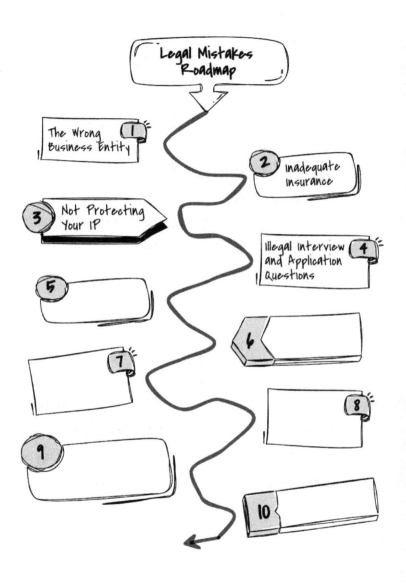

"I am convinced that nothing we do is more important than hiring and developing people. At the end of the day, you bet on people, not on strategies." Lawrence Bossidy; Author, and retired businessman.

"Acquiring the right talent is the most important key to growth... Hiring was – and still is – the most important thing we do." Marc Benioff; Founder, chairman, and CEO of Salesforce.

MISTAKE 4

USING ILLEGAL QUESTIONS ON JOB APPLICATIONS AND INTERVIEWS

An often-overlooked problem in hiring new employees is asking illegal questions on the job application and in the job interview. The law is clear: asking illegal questions on an application or in an interview can get you in trouble and possibly land you in court. Employers, whether a small local business or a large corporation, are required to adhere to certain federal and state laws. Not adhering to these laws could result in legal action and even criminal charges.

When we interview a job applicant, many of us start with small talk. It's an effort to help the applicant get comfortable and set the tone for the interview. One of my favorite, and light-hearted, initial interview questions is: Dunkin Donuts or Krispy Kreme? There is no wrong answer, but it does help get things started in a more comfortable tone!

While this light icebreaker question does not even go near the line of crossing over into illegal questions, many ice breaker questions can do just that. Questions such as: Are you married? Are you divorced? Do you have children? How old are your children? Where do you go to church?

These questions seem innocent enough as small talk goes, but they cross the line by asking for information that could be used to discriminate based on sex, age, or religion.

Let's discuss in more detail the types of questions we cannot ask on a job application or in an interview and the reasons and consider some alternate, acceptable questions.

There are several areas of questions you must be careful of when drafting a job application or interviewing applicants. All the areas are governed by laws that protect job applicants and employees against discrimination. The specific laws related to employment discrimination are covered later in this book in **Mistake 10 – Discrimination in Employment**.

Age Questions. It is *illegal* to ask: How old are you? What year were you born? When did you graduate from high school? It is *appropriate* to ask: Are you over the minimum age for the hours or working conditions? If the applicant is obviously over the minimum age to work, then there aren't any appropriate questions to ask related to age.

Disability Questions. It is *illegal* to ask: Do you have any disabilities: What is your medical history? How does your condition affect your abilities? An *appropriate* question to ask: Can you perform the specific tasks and duties of the job?

COVID-19 Vaccination Status. Asking questions about an applicant's vaccination status prior to hiring could be problematic. It might be used against you if that candidate is not hired for the position. Allegations of discrimination on a protected basis could arise from this line of questions. If vaccination is important to your business, you should have a written policy that applies equally to current employees and prospective employees. The policy should articulate how the requirement is job-related and a business necessity.

You may require vaccination after making the offer and before the new employee starts work. As long as you provide accommodations for employees requesting an exemption for disability or religious-related reasons. This requirement should be included in your job posting so that prospective employees are aware of the requirement prior to applying.

Criminal Record Questions. It is *illegal* to ask: Have you ever been arrested? Have you ever spent a night in jail? *Note*: There are exceptions if the applicant is being considered for a security-sensitive job and the employer can prove the conviction or history are related to the position.

Parental Status Questions. It is *illegal* to ask: How many children do you have? Do you plan to have children? How old are your children? Are you pregnant? Do you plan to become pregnant? What kind of childcare arrangements have you made? ***Appropriate*** questions to ask: Is there any reason you can't start at 7:30 a.m.? Can you work overtime? Questions about whether the applicant can meet specific work schedules or has activities or commitments that may prevent him or her from meeting attendance requirements are acceptable.

Gender-Related Questions. It is ***illegal*** to ask: What is your gender? Are you married? Are you divorced? Are you separated? Are you engaged? Are you widowed? Is this your maiden or married name? What is the name of your relative/spouse/children? Do you live with your parents? Questions concerning a spouse, or spouse's employment, salary, living arrangements, or dependents are not okay. How will your spouse feel about the amount of time you will be traveling if you get this job? ***Note***: It is illegal to require an applicant to provide a picture with their application.

Citizenship Questions. It is ***illegal*** to ask: Are you a U.S. citizen? Are your parents U.S. citizens? Is your spouse a U.S. citizen? On what date did you acquire U.S. citizenship? On what date did your parents acquire U.S. citizenship? On what date did your spouse acquire U.S. citizenship? Are you a naturalized or native-born U.S. citizen? Are your parents naturalized or native-born U.S. citizens? Is your spouse a naturalized or native-born U.S. citizen?

Appropriate questions to ask: Do you have the legal right to remain permanently in the U.S.? What is your visa status (if they answer no to the previous questions)? Are you able to provide proof of employment eligibility upon hire?

National Origin Questions. It is ***illegal*** to ask: What is your nationality? Where were you born? Where are your parents from? What is your heritage? How did you acquire the ability to speak, read, or write a foreign language? What language is spoken in your home? ***Appropriate*** questions to ask: What language do you speak, read, or write fluently? It is also appropriate to verify legal U.S. residence or work visa status.

Race or Skin Color Questions. It is ***illegal*** to ask: What race are you? Are you a member of a minority group? ***Note***: As mentioned previously, it is illegal to require an applicant to provide a picture with their application. ***Appropriate*** questions to ask: None.

Religion or Creed Questions. It is ***illegal*** to ask: What is your religious affiliation? Do you attend church regularly? What church do you attend? Which religious holidays will you be taking off from work? An ***appropriate*** question to ask: Can you work on Saturdays or Sundays?

Residence Questions. It is ***illegal*** to ask: Do you own or rent your home? Do you live in town?

Who do you live with? ***Appropriate*** questions to ask: Inquire about the best address to facilitate contact with the applicant. Will you be able to start work at 8:00 a.m.?

Education Questions. It is ***illegal*** to ask questions about an applicant's educational background if the job does not require a particular level of education. For example, asking about the English language proficiency and educational background of a secretarial applicant is proper, while the same questions would not be proper for a janitorial applicant.

Credit History and Garnishment Questions. It is ***illegal*** to ask: Have you ever had your wages garnished? Have you ever filed for bankruptcy? How is your credit rating? Do you own your own home?

Military Service Questions. It is ***illegal*** to ask: What type of discharge did you receive? Do you receive VA disability compensation? Do you have any health conditions from your military service? ***Appropriate*** questions to ask: What type of training did you receive? What was your Military Occupational Specialty (MOS)? Did you receive any specialized training? Where did you serve?

Before the interview, you should determine the questions you are going to ask the applicant. Make a written list of the questions and ask the same questions to all the applicants. Do not stray from the predetermined list of questions. You should bring the application and any other application documents, such as a resumé, to the interview. Review the application to confirm the information is correct and hasn't changed. Only the applicant should write on the application and any changes should be initialed by you and the applicant. Don't write notes or thoughts on the application itself. Keep your notes about the interview on a separate piece of paper.

If an applicant brings up any of the off-limits topics, gently move the discussion back to your list of questions. In your interview notes, comment on the applicant bringing up the off-limit topic and your response.

After hiring, there are questions you can ask that were not permitted during the interview process. When completing insurance forms, they may require proof of age and you can verify that information with a birth certificate or other identification. They may also require information about a new employee's medical history, dependent information, and marital status. Dependent information and marital status may also be required for tax forms. In this context, it is not illegal.

Always check with your lawyer for the latest restrictions imposed by your state. Please note, as always, these are just guidelines. Some questions may be acceptable depending on your situation.

If you are wondering what my answer to that hard-hitting interview question mentioned at the beginning of the chapter is; it used to be Dunkin Donuts until they stopped making the Toasted Coconut donut. Now I can't pass up a Krispy Kreme when the "Hot Now" sign is on!

Now that you know what you can and cannot ask in an interview, we will move on to the next mistake - **not having well-written agreements with your employees, suppliers, and customers.**

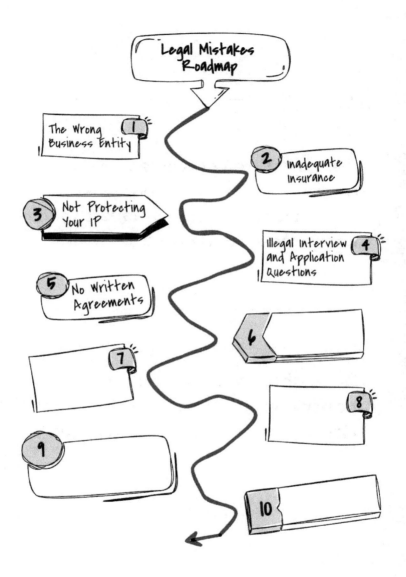

"With a written agreement you have a prayer; with a verbal agreement you have nothing but air." Robert Ringer; Entrepreneur and author.

"A verbal contract isn't worth the paper it's written on." Samuel Goldwyn; American Film Producer.

MISTAKE 5

NOT HAVING WELL-WRITTEN AGREEMENTS WITH EMPLOYEES, SUPPLIERS, AND CUSTOMERS

Many small business owners often neglect to have well-written agreements between employees, suppliers, and customers. This is often overlooked because the small business owner doesn't want to spend the money to have these documents drafted, especially when first starting. In the long run, investing in these agreements can save you time, money, and goodwill.

Employees

One of the most important documents for small businesses is the written employment contract. Even without a written employment agreement, a contract for employment is still formed and legally enforced. That is why it is important to have a well-written contract between the employer and the employee because it ensures that both the employer and the employee are aware and understand the terms and conditions of employment.

You should have a written agreement for all your employees; full-time, part-time, fixed-term, hourly, or salary. The agreement should be signed before the employee starts work and updated as needed over time. If the agreement is not signed before the employee starts work, some additional benefit (consideration) must be given, such as a signing bonus, promotion, or salary increase to make the agreement legally valid.

Employment agreements set out the terms and conditions of employment and any obligations that continue after the employment relationship ends, such as confidentiality and non-solicitation. They can limit a business's costs when terminating an employee. They also enhance the perceived value of the business to prospective buyers.

An employment agreement can be as simple or as complex as needed, depending on the type of employee. Hourly employees may only require a one-page letter detailing their wages, benefits, duties, at-will employment status, and termination provisions. Some items to consider including in the employment agreement are the type of employment (full-time, part-time, or fixed-term), start date, duties of the employee, rate of pay, hours of work, vacation entitlement, overtime entitlement, termination and resignation procedures, as well as post-employment obligations.

Salaried, commissioned, or professional employees will require a more detailed agreement. In addition to the basic information included in the hourly employee's agreement, agreements with these employees may include the term of the agreement, if for a defined amount of time; a dispute provision; termination resolution provision; attorney's fees provision; an applicable law section; and provisions governing confidentiality, non-compete, and non-solicitation. Additional sections may be needed depending on the specific job requirements. These more detailed agreements are best drafted by an attorney.

After signing the agreement, the employee should receive a copy of the agreement and a copy should be placed in their personnel file.

Suppliers/Vendors

Supplier agreements are between a business and its suppliers of services or goods. You may hear them called, "details of supply," "service contracts," "trade agreements," "schedule of services," or "details of service."

You should use, or require, a supplier agreement anytime you purchase products or services from another business. A well-thought-through agreement leads to a much better understanding between the owner and supplier. It references important milestones like the delivery date for goods and services and payment schedule. The terms and clauses will be different depending on the industry and products provided.

Some of the elements of a supplier agreement are the items the supplier must provide; the pricing and payments for the goods or services; expected time frames for work completion and payments; the responsibilities of each party; remedies in the event of a breach of the agreement; and the terms of the relationship.

If you want to charge the supplier for any attorney's fees and costs incurred should the supplier not perform as agreed and you must take them to court, the agreement must state that this will occur. Otherwise, you will most likely not be able to recover those fees.

A written agreement with a supplier is also an important method of establishing that the supplier is operating as an independent contractor. This would be helpful if you are audited by the IRS and need to prove their status using the 20-point test, as discussed later in **Mistake 7 – Improperly Classifying Employees as Independent Contractors**.

A signed written agreement is also legally necessary for specific types of deals in most states. The requirement of a signed written agreement is defined in the Statute of Frauds provisions of the Uniform Commercial Code. Typically, these are, (1) contracts for the sale of goods over $500, (2) agreements for the sale or transfer of real estate, (3) contracts, that by their terms, cannot be completed in one year, and (4) several other specific types of contracts.

Propriety information could be an important part of the agreement. If there are any trade secrets involved in your business, a confidentiality agreement, or clause, could be crucial to the continued safeguard of that information. Requiring a confidentiality agreement with your suppliers, manufacturers, or distributors ensures they do not share your trade secrets or formulas. If they do share this information, it provides a legal remedy to recover lost revenues in court.

Supplier agreements can be used in several ways such as outlining the provisions of service; proving the services an organization will provide to the business; information regarding the management and order fulfillment process for products or services; licensing agreements; rental agreements and the supply of rental items; leasing or franchising of equipment; and any aspect of the relationship between suppliers and your business. If there are any regulatory requirements, those should be included. Of course, I am going to mention the need for liability clauses to protect you should they be injured on your property, even though this should be covered by your liability insurance as discussed previously in **Mistake 2 – Not Having Adequate Insurance**.

Regardless of the monetary size of the transaction, to play it safe, put it in writing.

Customers

There are many benefits to having a written agreement with a customer. The first is it ensures everyone involved has a clear idea of the terms of their association. This helps avoid problems and misunderstandings. The next benefit is it creates documentation that can be used in the case of a lawsuit should the customer fail to pay or claim you did not perform as agreed. This protects you and your business in the future.

A customer agreement doesn't need to be a 20-page document filled with antiquated legal-sounding words like "wherefore," "hereto," and "herein." It can be as informal and as short or long as you want and need but it should include:

- the date the contract was executed or begins;
- the names of all the parties to the agreement using their full, legal name;
- the detailed scope of work, or what you will do for the customer, in as much detail as possible;

- who owns any intellectual property rights if you have a creative business;
- payment terms including the amount of down payment, incremental payments throughout the job, final payment amount, and total final cost;
- acceptable payment methods and any additional credit card fees;
- expiration date of the agreement;
- project deliverables;
- any deadlines, including milestones and final deliverables;
- how the agreement may be terminated by either party;
- how you will deal with delays;
- language regarding the working relationship as an independent contractor;
- remedies in case of breach of the agreement;
- possibly include an arbitration clause;
- attorney's fees provision;
- signature of both parties;
- and date of signing.

Depending on your business, you may be able to have an attorney draft a standard customer agreement you can use for all, or almost all, of your customers by simply filling in the blanks and crossing out unnecessary sections. In other types of business, a more detailed agreement, drafted for the specific client by an attorney may be necessary. Contract law is state-specific, so it is important to make sure your agreements conform to the laws of your state.

If your customer violates your agreement, there are several steps you can take to try and enforce it. Start with talking to the customer. Maybe they don't know they missed a payment or are merely running low on funds and hoped to get it caught up but didn't communicate with you. A polite reminder could be all it takes to get things back on track. If the customer refuses to honor the agreement, you should talk to a lawyer. They can review the agreement and advise you of your rights and next steps. If you included an arbitration clause, the next step may be moving forward with arbitration. If you don't have an arbitration clause, or arbitration fails, you will be forced to take them to court. If you end up in court, you will be grateful you invested in having an attorney draft an enforceable agreement.

Now that you have written agreements for your employees, suppliers, and customers we can look at the next legal mistake – **not having an employee handbook.**

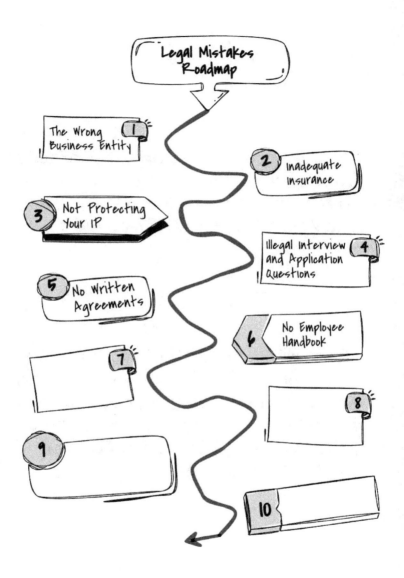

"Always treat your employees exactly as you want them to treat your best customers." Stephen R. Covey; Author, *The 7 Habits of Highly Effective People*.

"Research indicates that workers have three prime needs: Interesting work, recognition for doing a good job, and being let in on things that are going on in the company." Zig Zigler; Author and motivational speaker.

MISTAKE 6

NOT HAVING AN EMPLOYEE HANDBOOK

Every small business that has employees, regardless of how many or how few, should have an employee handbook. Your employees are the most important asset of your business, and the handbook sets out the rules, rights, and responsibilities that apply to employees of the business. Employee benefits such as vacation days, paid leave, health benefits, and insurance details are important topics to include in your handbook. A key purpose of your handbook is to ensure all employees are aware of these rights and benefits. It also puts in writing the company's culture, goals, and values. It is critical for building a solid employer-employee relationship and creating consistency within your organization.

An employee handbook is not a contract between the employer and the individual who is employed by the company. This is an important point to emphasize in your handbook. It is a useful tool in resolving workplace disputes and a valuable management tool, particularly for small businesses. It is inexpensive insurance to help decrease the likelihood of future litigation by disgruntled former employees. It provides legal evidence that rules, rights, and business practices were communicated to the employee, in writing, upon employment.

The topics that should be covered in an employee handbook are dependent on the type of business. They include:

Your Company Profile. Start with the mission of your business, explain what it is your company does, who it serves, and why. Include the history of your business and your business values and beliefs. Share your company vision and your goals for the company and how employees contribute to reaching those goals. The culture of the company, including any informal policies, should be shared.

Onboarding Guidelines. Your handbook should include information about what a new employee can expect as they begin work. It should include details of their position, team structure, and contact information for key personnel. If there is a trial or probation period, that should be included here. Explain the time system employees use and how hours are tracked. List the break and meal locations. Include all day-to-day things an employee needs to know for their workday.

Company Policies. Employees cannot meet your performance expectations if you don't tell them what they are. Your code of conduct should go here. Make clear what is acceptable behavior during company time. List the daily work hours for employees in the office and any policies about remote work or flexible hours. Give expectations for attendance including policies for tardiness and leaving early. This section may include a dress code to ensure everyone looks professional or at least complies with the company's standards. Provide the policy for taking time off for vacation or sick leave. List any company paid holidays provided. Tell employees your policy for the length and frequency of breaks and mealtimes. Make sure your break policy complies with any state-mandated requirements. In Illinois, an employee must be given a meal period of at least 20 minutes if they are scheduled to work 7.5 continuous hours or more. It must be given no later than five hours after beginning work. Your drug-free and alcohol-free workplace policy and smoking policy would be included in this section. Any activities that can get an employee disciplined should be listed in this section.

Social Media Policy. I split this out from the general company policy paragraph because in the social media-driven society we live in today it requires a longer discussion. The first thing to understand is that you cannot control or restrict what an employee posts on their personal social media accounts on their own time outside of work hours.

However, you can limit an employee's use of social media on company time even on personal devices. If you choose to limit the use of personal devices, the policy should be clear and uniformly enforced.

As you consider the language of your social media policy, keep in mind the value of your employee's social media network to your business. Positive company culture determines many of the outcomes of a social media policy. Happy employees can be some of your best marketers by sharing their experience at your business and your great products or services.

As part of the policy, emphasize any confidentiality requirements relating to clients or products. Define what is acceptable public information and what is not. Employees should be educated about how to provide disclaimers in any of their politically motivated posts. You cannot limit what they say, but you can ask that they add language in their posts that their views are not necessarily the views of their employer.

Your policy should also include how company-owned social media accounts are managed and used. Assign roles, develop security protocols, create a social media response plan, and ensure its use complies with state and federal laws.

Compensation and Performance Reviews. Include the payroll schedule and payment options. You should also discuss what deductions are taken from your employees' checks. If workers are required to travel for business, then you'll need to cover the travel and expenses policy. Include job classification details, promotion process, and job transfer process. Outline the performance review process including the frequency of reviews and standards of performance.

Benefits. All benefits you offer should be listed including retirement plans, health insurance, life insurance, disability insurance, and workers' compensation insurance.

Safety Guidelines. This section provides the policies in place for emergencies, health, and safety purposes. This includes safety procedures that outline what to do in the event someone is injured on the job. The location of the first aid kit, fire extinguishers, and other key tools is essential. If employees drive company vehicles, then the standard procedures for reporting accidents should be explained.

Legal Requirements. It is important to state that the handbook is not a contract and reinforce their employment-at-will status. If your business has 50 or more employees, include information about the Family Medical Leave Act (FMLA). Include workers' compensation policy information and what happens if an employee is hurt on the job. You should include a non-discrimination, anti-harassment, and equal opportunity policy. You must discuss how you accommodate people with disabilities in your workplace. Explain that the policies in the handbook are subject to change at any time and they will be notified of any changes. Tell them where you post the state and federally required notices in your business location. The handbook should include a form verifying the employee read and understands the information contained in the Employee Handbook. It should also include other documents you use that require a signature such as the at-will employment clause, conflict of interest statement, confidentiality agreement, non-compete, non-solicitation, and equal employment opportunity statement. A copy of the signed and dated documents should be given to the employee and a copy kept in their personnel file.

Appropriate Use of Company Equipment. Many businesses rely heavily on computers in their day-to-day operations. It is important to put in writing your policy for the personal use of business computers. If you do not want your employees checking and sending personal emails and using the internet to check social media feeds on your computers, then put that in writing. Your policy on making personal phone calls on business phones or using their cell phone while on company times should be addressed. If you are more flexible in your tolerance for these activities, you should discuss your expectations to give employees an idea of what is permissible. Provide the policy for the personal use of the company car.

Discipline and Termination. You must clearly define the infractions that require disciplinary steps. It should explain each step in the progressive discipline process and how the last step leads to termination of employment. This section should include the information discussed in **Mistake 9 – Not Properly Counseling and Terminating Employees**.

Employee Problem Resolution Procedures. Include the formal process for employees to report internal complaints or grievances if they believe they need to seek fair treatment.

Your Employee Handbook does not have to include all these sections or use these titles. These are suggestions for some of the information you could include. There is also more information that could be included depending on how detailed you want to make this document. However, there are some sections, such as the ones listed in the Legal Requirements paragraph, you should include.

You should review your employee handbook annually to make sure it complies with state and federal laws. An annual review also provides an opportunity to update your handbook to keep up with societal changes or changes in company policy.

If changes are made to the handbook, employees must sign a new acknowledgment that they have read the handbook. Even if no changes are made to the handbook, it is a good policy to have employees reread and resign the acknowledgment annually.

If you cannot afford to have an attorney draft your Employee Handbook initially, you can find many examples of Employee Handbooks through a quick search of the internet. It is easy to get overwhelmed with the number of samples available. Select one basic template that covers most of the information I suggest here and begin with that. Revise the sample handbook using language that reflects your company style and culture. The rules you have for your employees and how you relay them is another way you set the tone of your leadership of the company.

After you have drafted your Employee Handbook, I would recommend you have an attorney review it. This should be less costly than drafting a complete handbook and will ensure you have the necessary legal language to minimize your liabilities.

Now with your Employee Handbook in place, we move to the next mistake – **improperly classifying employees as independent contractors.**

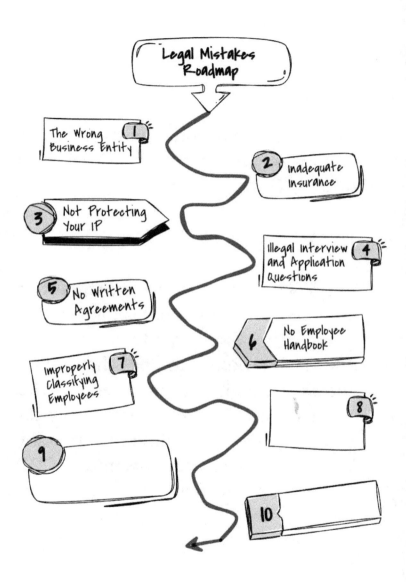

"People are not your most important asset. The right people are." Jim Collins; Author, *Good to Great*.

"Employees are a company's greatest asset — They're your competitive advantage. You want to attract and retain the best; provide them with encouragement, stimulus, and make them feel that they are an integral part of the company's mission." Anne M. Mulcahy; former chairperson and CEO of Xerox Corporation.

MISTAKE 7

IMPROPERLY CLASSIFYING EMPLOYEES AS INDEPENDENT CONTRACTORS

Many small businesses incorrectly classify employees as independent contractors. This mistake can cost your business money in back wages and penalties. There are several factors the federal government uses to determine whether someone is an independent contractor or an employee. We will look at those factors in detail and offer some suggestions to avoid the tax problems of misclassifying employees as contractors.

An independent contractor is an individual that works for themselves. They are not employed by another entity and have more independence than an employee would. They have control over all aspects of the job, from what they do to how they do it. Independent contractors typically provide their own equipment and supplies, as well as set their own hours. Independent contractors are often hired to work on an hourly basis but can also be paid one flat rate for a job.

An employee is typically a worker who has a contract with an employer and receives a set wage or salary and may receive benefits. The employee must conduct their work in the location determined by the employer. The employer typically provides the employee with a work uniform, equipment, and supplies. An important factor in whether an independent contractor relationship exists is the right to control the manner and means of performance. The more control an employer has over the worker, the more likely that worker is an employee.

IRS 20-Factor Test

The IRS uses twenty factors to determine whether someone is an independent contractor or an employee. No single factor controls the determination of the worker's status. Let's look at each factor and see how they might apply to your business.

Instructions. Is the worker required to comply with the employer's instructions about when, where, and how to work?

Training. Is training required? Does the worker receive training from or at the direction of the employer, including attending meetings and working with experienced employees?

Integration. Are the worker's services integrated with the activities of the company? Does the success of the employer's business significantly depend upon the performance of services provided by the worker?

Services Rendered Personally. Is the worker required to perform the work personally? Can they subcontract out the work to be performed?

Authority to hire, supervise, and pay assistants. Does the worker have the ability to hire, supervise, and pay assistants for the employer?

Continuing Relationship. Does the worker have a continuing relationship with the employer?

Set Hours of Work. Is the worker required to follow set hours of work?

Full-time Work Required. Does the worker work full-time for the employer?

Place of Work. Does the worker perform work on the employer's premises and use the company's office equipment?

Sequence of Work. Does the worker perform work in a sequence prescribed by the employer? Does the worker follow a set schedule?

Reporting Obligations. Does the worker submit regular written or oral reports to the employer?

Method of Payment. How does the worker receive payments? Are there payments of regular amounts at set intervals?

Payment of Business and Travel Expenses. Does the worker receive payments to reimburse them for business and travel expenses?

Furnishing of Tools and Materials. Does the worker rely on the employer for tools and materials?

Investment. Has the worker invested in the facilities or equipment used to perform the services?

Risk of Loss. Is the payment made to the worker on a fixed basis regardless of the profitability or loss of the business?

Working for More Than One Company at a Time. Does the worker only work for one employer at a time?

Availability of Services to the General Public. Are the services offered to the employer unavailable to the general public?

Right to Discharge. Can the worker be fired by the employer?

Right to Quit. Can the worker quit work at any time without liability?

If you answered many of these questions with "yes," you most likely have an employer-employee relationship. If most of your answers are "no," you could have an independent contractor relationship.

You cannot contract away a worker's status as an employee. Just because you say someone is an independent contractor, or even have a signed contract that says they are an independent contractor, does not mean those workers are independent contractors for IRS purposes. The 20-factor duties test listed above overrides any contract you may have with an employee.

The Dangers of Misclassifying Employees as Independent Contractors

Some employers intentionally misclassify employees as independent contractors to avoid paying minimum wage, overtime compensation, worker's compensation, and other obligations to workers. Employers do not withhold federal, state, and local taxes from wages paid to independent contractors. They are not included in an employer's benefits programs, are exempt from wage and hour and employment discrimination laws, and unemployment insurance. In the short run, these are savings to the employer.

Even though the immediate costs of having an employee can be costlier than paying them as independent contractors; the long-term costs, if the IRS finds out you misclassified an employee as an independent contractor, will be much more. Penalties can include back taxes or premiums, civil fines, interest, other retroactive damages, and even attorney's fees to defend you against government agencies or civil lawsuits.

If you are paying workers as independent contractors who should be paid as employees, I encourage you to "hire" them legally and properly. It is a business risk to continue paying them as independent contractors and as a business owner, you should attempt to limit as many risks as you have under your control.

If you would like a printable copy of the IRS 20-factor test, I included one in the resource material that accompanies this book. You can get it at this link:

LegalAdvocacyHeadquarters.com/resources

Password: LAHQResources

Now that you understand the proper classification of your employees, we will look at the next mistake - **not paying your employees properly.**

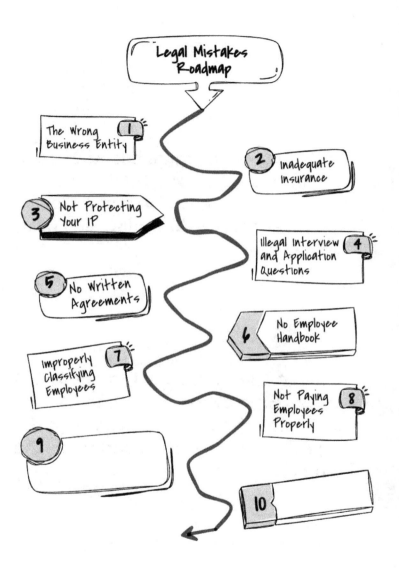

"I don't pay good wages because I have a lot of money; I have a lot of money because I pay good wages." Robert Bosch; German industrialist, engineer, and inventor.

"It is not the employer that pays the wages. Employers only handle the money. It is the customer who pays the wages." Henry Ford; founder of the Ford Motor Company.

MISTAKE 8

IMPROPERLY PAYING EMPLOYEES

Another legal mistake made by entrepreneurs is not paying their employees properly. This happens in several ways. One of the ways is simply not paying your employees for the work they perform. Another way is not paying the proper minimum wage. Closely tied to not paying minimum wage is not paying overtime. Although not a pay issue, but rather a deduction/submission issue; not withholding the appropriate amounts from employee paychecks and not submitting the proper taxes to the IRS can also land you in trouble with the IRS. Additionally, not properly classifying and paying exempt, or salaried, employees could put you on the wrong side of a wage and salary audit by a government agency. If you do not pay employees properly, you could be liable for back wages, interest, fines and penalties, and attorney's fees.

Not Paying Workers

This may seem like an obvious point, so I will get it out of the way first. Generally, you must pay wages to anyone who works for you. Period. Under the Fair Labor Standards Act (FLSA) and most state laws, employees may not volunteer their services to a for-profit private sector business. There are some exceptions, but those are best discussed with your attorney. Even if your employee says they want to do it and you have a good relationship with that employee, don't do it. Positive working relationships are good until they aren't. Department of Labor audits aren't started by employees who are happy with their boss.

I represented an employee who worked full-time for her employer for six months. She kept track of her hours by writing them in a spiral notebook. Her employer initially paid her some of her wages, but the business was just starting out and the employer couldn't pay her all her wages. After about a month, the owner stopped paying her anything. Promising to make it up to her when business improved. The employee wanted to help her boss out, so she continued to work for her for another four months or so, without receiving any pay. The business closed after six months, and my client was out of a job. Not the worst thing since she wasn't being paid. She talked to her boss about her back wages, but her boss was unable and unwilling to pay her. The owner said the employee had volunteered to work for the business, so the owner didn't owe her the back wages. The employee hired me to represent her, and we filed in small claims court. The business owner got a lawyer but was unable to pay when the case drug out and decided to represent herself. The initial amount of the back wages owed was $5,822. On the day of the final hearing, we settled the case for $14,678. Almost triple the amount of the original back pay claim. That total amount included the statutory allowance for damages and interest of $2,678, attorney's fees of $6,178, as provided by the statute, and the back wages.

As you can see, this mistake can cost you a lot of money in back wages, interest, penalties, and attorney's fees for your attorney and the employee's attorney. The Illinois Wage Payment and Collections Act is a very strict statute and even includes criminal charges associated with the willful refusal to pay wages. Don't do it.

Minimum Wage

The federal minimum wage is currently $7.25 an hour. However, in some states, the minimum wage is higher than that: $14 an hour in California, $11 an hour in Arkansas, $13.20 an hour in New York, and $14.25 an hour in Massachusetts. The current minimum wage in Illinois is $12.00. The minimum wage in Illinois will increase by $1.00 per year until reaching the rate of $15.00 an hour in 2025.

If employees in your business receive gratuities, you may pay them 60% of the minimum wage. To be properly classified as a tipped employee, the employee must receive $20 a month or more in tips. The rules in this section are governed by the Illinois Minimum Wage Law, 820 ILCS 105.

Overtime Pay

Overtime pay is generally paid to non-exempt employees for hours worked over 40 hours per week. If an employee works overtime, the employee will be compensated by overtime pay. The FLSA sets an overtime pay rate that is calculated by multiplying the regular hourly rate by 1.5 by the number of hours worked over 40 hours. For example, Joe works an hourly job subject to overtime laws. His regular hourly pay is $12.00. The first week of the month he works 47 hours at the job. His pay for the week before taxes, including overtime, is $606. We get that by multiplying his regular hourly rate of $12.00 by 40 hours to get $480. Then we multiply his regular rate of $12.00 by the statutory multiplier of 1.5 to get the overtime rate of $18.00 an hour. Then we multiply the overtime rate of $18.00 an hour by the number of overtime hours - 7 – to get his overtime pay: $126. We then add the overtime pay of $126 to his regular pay of $480 to get $606.

There are other ways to compute overtime for employees that are not paid an hourly rate. There are calculations for workers paid on a piece-rate basis; paid day rates or by the job; on a weekly salary basis;

a salary for a period other than a workweek; a fixed salary for work hours that fluctuate from week to week; in a single workweek is paid two or more different rates; receives payments other than cash; or works on a commission. Each of these different compensation methods has its method for calculating overtime. In Illinois, if you pay any of your employees in one or more of these ways, you should look at the Illinois Administrative Code, Title 56, Chapter I(b) Part 210.430, Methods of Computing Overtime.

The workweek is defined as a fixed and regularly occurring period. It consists of seven consecutive 24-hour periods. Once you determine the beginning day and time of the workweek for your business, it remains fixed. You can't change it week to week, or month to month, to attempt to avoid paying overtime. The calculation of overtime hours starts from the beginning day and time of your workweek. Most business's work weeks start on Monday, however, if your business doesn't open until Tuesday or Wednesday, you may prefer to start the week on one of those days. If you do not establish a defined workweek, the Illinois Department of Labor will consider a calendar week as your workweek. It is the seven-day period beginning at 12:01 a.m. Sunday morning until the following Saturday night at midnight.

Withholding and Paying Taxes

As a small business owner, you are required to pay your portion of taxes for your employees and to withhold the employee's portion of taxes. You are then required to submit those taxes, your portion and theirs, to the IRS. This is not a section on what taxes you must pay and withhold, nor the filing requirements. This is just a strong warning not to mess this up, intentionally or unintentionally. This one mistake can cost you significantly. Al Capone wasn't charged with crimes related to his various illegal activities, but he was indicted and convicted for tax evasion. The IRS website has some great resources for small business owners. If you don't have the time, patience, or interest to learn what you need to do, then get professional assistance from a good bookkeeper or accountant.

https://www.irs.gov/businesses

Exempt Employees

If an employee is classified as an "exempt" employee, you don't have to pay them overtime for hours worked above 40 hours. To be classified as an exempt employee you must pay them a salary of at least $684 a week ($35,568 a year) or an hourly rate of $27.63 or more, and they must perform exempt job duties. To meet the salary basis requirement, you must guarantee your employee the minimum salary ($684 a week) for any workweek they do any work for you. You do not need to pay your exempt employees during any week they do not do any work for you. An exception to this would be paid vacation you provide as an employee benefit.

Exempt job duties are relatively high-level work. They are classified into three different types of duties: executive, professional, or administrative.

Executive. The employee must be responsible for supervising at least two other full-time employees. Or the equivalent in part-time employees. They must be employees, not volunteers or interns. The primary duty of the job must be management. Management duties include interviewing and training new employees, maintaining records, handling employee grievances, planning work for their department, delegating work, budget plans, and other managerial tasks. You must give them some input into job status decisions, such as hiring, firing, promotions, or assignments.

Professional. The job duties of the traditional "learned professionals" are exempt. These include lawyers, doctors, dentists, teachers, architects, registered nurses, accountants, engineers, actuaries, pharmacists, and clergy. Professionally exempt employees must have education beyond high school, and usually beyond a college degree, in fields that are distinguished from the mechanical arts or skilled trades.

Administrative. This is the most difficult to define. The FLSA defines exempt administrative job duties as:

(a) Office or nonmanual work, which is
(b) directly related to management or general business operations of the employer or the employer's customers, and
(c) a primary component of which involves the exercise of independent judgment and discretion about
(d) matters of significance.

This exemption is for employees who:

1. "keep the business running."
2. exercise discretion and independent judgment in their job.
3. provide support to the operational or production employees.
4. are considered "staff" rather than "line" employees.
5. are not clerical or secretarial positions.
6. must be allowed to make important decisions as a regular part of their job.

Some examples of exempt functional areas include "tax; finance; accounting; budgeting;

auditing; insurance; quality control; purchasing; procurement; advertising; marketing; research; safety and health; personnel management; human resources; employee benefits; labor relations; public relations; government relations; computer network; internet and database administration; legal and regulatory compliance; and similar activities." *See* Department of Labor Fact Sheet 17C.

Even if you give an employee a title that sounds managerial or supervisory, the actual duties the employee performs are what determine whether the employee is an exempt employee. As with many of these legal mistakes, improperly classifying your employees as exempt can cost you money in unpaid overtime and possibly fines and legal fees. The Department of Labor website has several good resources to assist you in making the proper determination.

https://www.dol.gov/agencies/whd/overtime/fact-sheets

Now that you are prepared to properly pay your employees, let's discuss the mistake of **not properly counseling and terminating employees.**

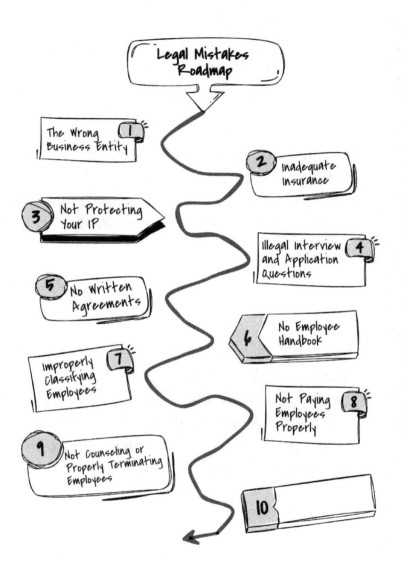

"Dealing with employee issues can be difficult, but NOT dealing with them can be worse." Paul Foster; CEO and Founder, The Business Therapist.

"It's not the people you fire who make your life miserable. It's the people you don't." Dick Grote; Author, *Discipline Without Punishment: The Proven Strategy That Turns Problem Employees into Superior Performers.*

MISTAKE 9

NOT PROPERLY COUNSELING AND TERMINATING EMPLOYEES

Hiring and firing employees is difficult, but sometimes a necessary part of small business ownership. As the owner, and leader, of your business you bear the responsibility of creating and molding your company's culture. A culture that can be impacted negatively or positively by how you handle the performance of your employees. The key to making the management of your employees, including firing, easier is to have defined expectations and set steps for performance improvement before termination.

Performance Improvement Plans

Sometimes an employee intentionally, or unintentionally breaks your rules as set out in your Employee Handbook. (You have an Employee Handbook, don't you? If not, reread **Mistake 5** and get one in place!) They regularly arrive late, consistently forget to clock in, or take too long a lunch break. Other times an employee isn't meeting performance expectations. They are rude to customers on the phone, are not keeping their assigned work area clean enough, or aren't producing the amount of work you require from them. In situations like these, you need to counsel that employee in writing, so they are put on notice of the rule they are breaking or the performance measure they are not meeting. This is best done through a written progressive employee Performance Improvement Plan.

A Performance Improvement Plan (PIP) is an agreement between the employee and employer that describes the identified infraction or performance shortfall, the performance goals the employee must meet to keep their job, how long they must complete them, and what happens if they fail to meet these goals. A PIP should include job responsibilities, work schedule, direct supervisor and manager contact information, performance standards and expected results, times, and locations for meetings to discuss progress and support, who will be responsible for the completion of the goals, consequences for failing to meet the goals, and expected timeline.

The plan should not be created in haste but should be well defined and have timeframes that can be followed. If you have a clear plan with defined goals, your employees will feel better than if you provide vague demands for improvement and no clear path to success.

When you first notice the performance issue, it is important to begin writing everything down. If you don't write it down, it didn't happen. Even documenting informal conversations can be important if piecing together a timeline or reminding yourself of them become necessary in the future. If possible, collect copies of electronic communications such as email or text messages. Notes about phone conversations, one-on-one conversations, or impressions of watching unprofessional or subpar behavior in interactions with co-workers or groups.

The keys to an effective PIP are written expectations and consistency. With no set goals and no written plan, it is impossible to have regular reviews and positive and negative consequences for success or failure. The PIP should be given to the employee in person and in private. It is a good idea to have a witness present, typically the employee's supervisor or a manager. The PIP should be signed by the employee and their manager or supervisor, and a copy given to the employee.

Here are five mistakes to avoid in implementing a performance improvement plan. The **first** mistake is not addressing the specific problem areas, such as spending too much time on tasks or social media usage.

The **second** mistake is not holding employees accountable for their actions. For example, not following through on warnings given in the plan. This leads to failure and discourages employees from participating meaningfully in the program.

The **third** mistake is not having a manager or supervisor available to participate in the plan. The manager or supervisor can help employees understand what they are expected to do and make sure they do not forget or misunderstand. Employees may not be completely committed to the changes required if they do not know what is expected of them.

The **fourth** mistake is not giving your employees the tools and support to succeed. Employees need management to hold them accountable and provide them with training and resources. If an employee's performance is not meeting expectations, determine whether there is additional training you can provide that will help them do their job better.

The **fifth** mistake is not assessing the effectiveness of the program. PIPs must be measured to determine the effectiveness of the plan. For example, managers should monitor each employee's behavior regularly to see if their performance has improved.

While a plan to improve performance may help motivate your employee and get them back on track, an effective employee improvement plan may also save you from potential lawsuits. Written documentation of an employee's performance shortfalls, your efforts to help the employee improve their performance, and their inability or unwillingness to improve will be very helpful should a fired employee attempt to sue you for wrongful termination.

Sometimes, an employee's performance is not improving despite your best attempts to help them. For these instances, you may need to terminate the employee.

Terminating Employees

Terminating an employee is not always easy but is sometimes necessary for the efficiency and well-being of your company. It can also be the best thing for an employee when the job isn't a good fit for them or you. Terminating an employee that isn't a good fit frees them to find the job that is a better fit for them.

Employee termination procedures are formal, documented processes for the dismissal of an employee. They are usually spelled out in the employee policy manual or Employee Handbook. (Do I need to nudge you again toward having an Employee Handbook? *See* **Mistake 5**.) Employee termination procedures should include the following: the reasons for termination; whether the termination is final; whether the termination is based on performance, conduct, or other causes; an appeal process if any; and the employee's rights as a former employee. The reasons for termination should indicate whether the employee has been given the opportunity to improve through a PIP.

The laws regarding the reasons an employer may terminate an employee are state-specific, however, the majority of states are "employment-at-will" states. Illinois is an "employment-at-will" state. You can terminate an employee for any reason, or no reason, without any notice. As long as it is not one of the discriminatory reasons I discuss in the next chapter: **Mistake 10 – Discrimination in Employment**.

If you have an agreement with an employee that has a termination provision that gives the conditions for termination, you may not be able to terminate that employee without a reason or notice, except for cause. You will be required to follow the terms set out in your agreement with that employee.

It is important an employee is terminated properly and there is a plan in place for the termination process. Because terminating someone has significant legal implications, you should consult with a lawyer before beginning the process of terminating an employee. If you do not have a plan in place, you may face potential lawsuits for wrongful termination. You should communicate with the employee and be sure the employee understands the reasons for termination before you implement the plan. The plan should be communicated to the employee when they are notified of their termination.

Make sure you follow a documented, formal plan for termination. When terminating an employee, follow these steps to make sure the employee has a clear understanding of the process.

Suggested steps to a successful termination:

1. Complete a thorough review of the PIP.
2. Create a letter of termination.
3. Schedule a meeting with the employee and have at least one witness present.
4. Inform the employee they will be terminated.
5. Inform them of their rights.
6. Discuss how the termination will be communicated to co-workers.
7. Provide the employee an opportunity to ask questions and confirm their understanding of the process.
8. Sign the letter of termination and have the employee sign.
9. Provide a copy of the letter to the terminated employee.
10. Accompany the employee while cleaning out their workspace.
11. Terminate any electronic access to company computers or information systems.
12. Collect their employee ID, building key, and any other company property.
13. Comply with all state and federal laws regarding severance or last payments owed.

14. Depending on the circumstances, you might consider changing the locks on entry doors.
15. Transfer the employee's necessary work responsibilities to another person.

The employee should be given a written letter notifying them they are being terminated and it can include the reasons for termination. It can be titled, "Termination Letter," "Notice of Termination," "Employment Separation Letter," or any similar title. The Termination Letter should include details of the employee's dismissal. Include the name of the employee, their title or position, and the name and contact information of the manager or HR person in charge of the process. If for cause, you can provide a description of the event or events that resulted in the decision to terminate the employee. Include information from the performance improvement plan or include a copy of it. List when any benefits will end, including health benefits or insurance. Provide details about any severance pay, final paycheck, or payout of vacation time, if applicable. List the employee's termination date. Include a reminder to the employee they are required to return any company property they may have in their possession. Have the employee sign a copy of the letter and keep it in their personnel file for future reference if needed. If the employee refuses to sign, note that as well.

I included a sample copy of a Termination Letter in the resource material.

Properly terminating an employee is an important part of maintaining your company culture and mitigating the potential for future lawsuits. Creating a written process for improvement as well as termination will prepare you for the inevitable employee performance issue. This is another area I strongly suggest you get assistance from a lawyer in drafting your PIP and termination process. If you don't have an HR department, guidance from a lawyer before and during the actual termination process is money well spent in mitigating future liabilities that could arise from a wrongful termination lawsuit.

Now that you have a plan in place to properly counsel and terminate underperforming or rule-breaking employees, we will look at our last mistake – **discrimination in employment**.

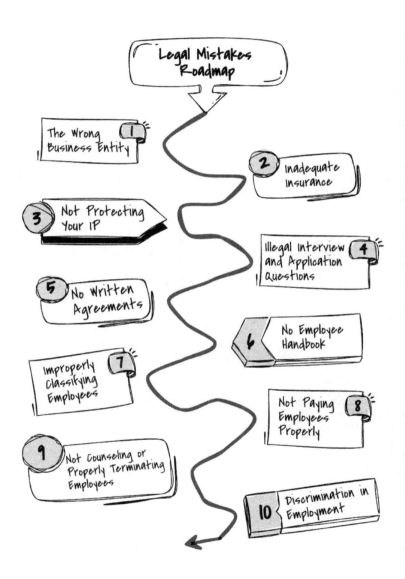

"Discrimination, in all its forms, is bad for business." Tim Cook; CEO of Apple.

MISTAKE 10

DISCRIMINATION IN EMPLOYMENT

Even small business owners must be aware of instances of employment discrimination in the workplace. No small business, regardless of how small, is exempt from all employment discrimination laws. Consciously and unconsciously, discrimination can occur among owners and employees. As the business owner, you must set the tone in your company and not allow discrimination of any type. Regardless of who in your organization perpetrates the discrimination, you are ultimately responsible, and your business is legally liable for those actions. The first step in combating this challenge is awareness and education.

Employment discrimination is the unfair treatment of an individual or a group of individuals based on their race, color, ethnic or national origin, language, age, religion, sex, sexual orientation, military service, or disability status. Employment discrimination occurs when an employer makes decisions or provides or withholds opportunities based on a protected characteristic. Federal and state laws also protect workers from retaliation for reporting instances of discrimination against themselves or participating in a claim or investigation.

Employment discrimination can occur in many forms, including hiring, firing, promotion decisions, pay, or benefits. It may also take the form of harassing or abusive workplace conditions.

Employment discrimination can be overt or covert. Overt discrimination is when the decision is based on a protected characteristic and is publicly communicated. It is an explicit display of unequal treatment of an individual or group because of a protected characteristic they possess. Overt discrimination may include a boss who tells a female employee that women don't make good managers and when she later applies for a promotion to manager, a less qualified man is selected. Covert discrimination is when there are no apparent or communicated signs of discrimination, but the protected characteristic is a factor in the decision. A well-qualified Army National Guard soldier applies for a promotion and a less qualified candidate with fewer years at the company is given the promotion instead. The supervisor has never publicly said anything about the Soldier's service but harbors resentment toward the soldier because he must cover the soldier's shifts on drill weekends when they are at training. He complains about covering the shifts although he doesn't state the reason. Covert discrimination can be difficult, but not impossible to prove. Employment discrimination is most likely to occur when someone is new to a workplace, either as an applicant or as a newly hired worker.

There are federal and state laws that cover employment discrimination.

Federal Laws

Title VII of the Civil Rights Act of 1964. This Act makes it illegal to discriminate against someone based on race, religion, national origin, or sex. This includes refusing to hire someone for any of these reasons. In June 2020, the U.S. Supreme Court held that an "employer who fires an individual merely for being gay or transgender violates Title VII" of the Civil Rights Act. Title VII applies to businesses with 15 or more employees.

The Pregnancy Discrimination Act. This Act amended Title VII to expand the protections regarding "sex" to include prohibiting sex discrimination based on pregnancy, childbirth, or a medical condition related to pregnancy or childbirth. This Act applies to businesses with 15 or more employees.

The Equal Pay Act of 1963 (EPA). It prohibits sex-based wage discrimination between men and women who perform equal work in the same workplace. The Equal Pay Act applies to employers with any number of employees.

The Age Discrimination in Employment Act of 1967 (ADEA). This act protects employees or job candidates who are 40 or older from discrimination in the workplace. This law applies to businesses with 20 or more employees.

Title I of the Americans with Disabilities Act of 1990 (ADA). Makes it illegal to discriminate against a qualified person with a disability in the process of employment or during employment. It requires employers to make reasonable accommodations in working conditions for employees with disabilities. The ADA applies to businesses with 15 or more employees.

Uniformed Services Employment and Reemployment Rights Act (USERRA). This Act makes it illegal for employers to deny employment, or terminate employment, of a current or former service member because of his or her obligations to the military. USERRA applies to businesses with any number of employees.

These laws form the basis of how the Equal Employment Opportunity Commission (EEOC) enforces employment discrimination complaints. Federal courts interpret these laws on an ongoing basis. Additionally, each state has its employment discrimination laws and enforcement agencies to investigate and prosecute claims of employment discrimination.

State Laws

In Illinois, the Illinois Human Rights Act (IHRA) prohibits discrimination in employment, real estate transactions including rentals, financial credit, public accommodations, housing, sexual harassment, and sexual harassment in education. The IHRA provides broader protections than the federal laws by including additional protected classes. It prohibits discrimination based on race, color, religion, sex, national origin, citizenship status, criminal history, ancestry, age, order of protection status, marital status, physical or mental disability, military status, sexual orientation, gender identity, pregnancy, sexual harassment, and unfavorable discharge from military service. The IHRA also prohibits retaliation against anyone who opposes discriminatory treatment or participates in an investigation of discriminatory treatment. *See* Illinois Human Rights Act, 775 ILCS 5.

Unlike most of the federal laws that prohibit discrimination, the IHRA applies to "any person employing one or more employees within Illinois during 20 or more calendar weeks within the calendar year." IHRA, 775 ILCS 5/2-101(B). This is an important difference as even the smallest of small businesses are included in this law.

Prevention

After becoming educated about the laws that prohibit discrimination, the next step is to prevent discrimination from occurring in your business. This begins with a zero-tolerance policy for your company. Although "zero-tolerance" may seem harsh, discrimination in your business is a serious matter and should not be taken lightly. Your company culture should encourage employees to respect each other's differences and show them how those differences make your organization stronger.

You should have a policy that is firm and documented in your employee handbook. Although discrimination based on sex includes sexual harassment, include a separate written policy against sexual harassment. Unfortunately, instances of sexual harassment in the workplace are prevalent enough to warrant its own policy.

Train your employees in the laws regarding discrimination and the consequences of violating those laws. Show them how to report instances of discrimination to their supervisor or human resources. An inclusive culture will help them not feel intimidated or afraid to report the activity. Train new employees upon being hired and provide regular training throughout their time with your company. Train supervisors and managers on how to conduct proper employment reviews that objectively document their employees' strengths and weaknesses. Also train them how to properly handle complaints of discrimination, sexual harassment, or requests for reasonable accommodations for disabilities.

You should be vigilant in the day-to-day operations of your business for any evidence of inappropriate behavior. If you see or hear it before someone complains, take swift action to stop the offending behavior. Investigate complaints of discrimination or sexual harassment promptly, confidentially, and thoroughly. The investigation should be documented, and if the complaint is found to have merit, corrective action should be taken. The level of discipline required for each incident will depend on the severity of the action, past behavior, and willingness to change. It is important to be consistent in the enforcement of these policies.

As the owner, you also have the responsibility to provide employees with disabilities a reasonable accommodation in working conditions if that employee requests an accommodation. Not all accommodations can be provided, but you must have a discussion with the employee to try and find some way to accommodate their disability through adjustments to the duties of the job or where and how the job is performed. Some examples of reasonable accommodations include modifying job duties; restructuring work sites; providing flexible work schedules; providing accessible technology or other adaptive equipment.

This is another area that assistance from an attorney is a good investment in mitigating risk and protecting your business. An attorney can assist in drafting your discrimination and sexual harassment policies, as well as advise you on proper investigation procedures or conduct the investigation themself, and disciplinary action if needed. They can also advise you during the interactive process of finding a mutually agreeable accommodation for employees with disabilities.

Now that you have added knowledge of the laws related to employment discrimination to the other information you learned in this short book, you are better prepared to avoid these ten mistakes.

But before you go, I want to share how I can help you **proactively protect your business.**

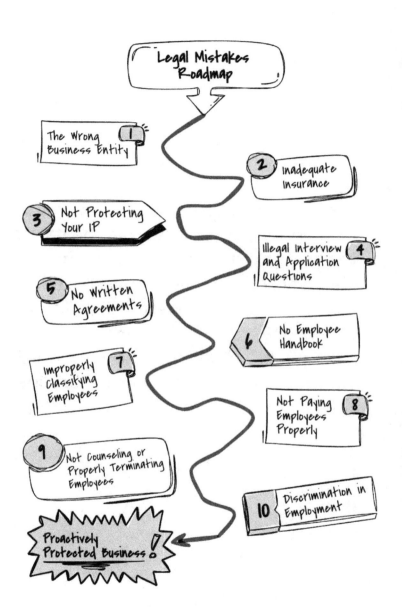

"Fix the basics, protect first what matters for your business and be ready to react properly to pertinent threats. Think data, but also business services integrity, awareness, customer experience, compliance, and reputation." Stephane Nappo; Chief Information Security Officer, Groupe SEB.

HOW I HELP ENTREPRENEURS PROACTIVELY PROTECT THEIR SMALL BUSINESSES

Many business owners don't spend the money upfront when starting their business to do many of the things discussed in this book. I get it. When you are first starting, you typically have more time than money, so you invest your money in inventory, machinery, or a building and spend the time you have on getting it all going in the right direction. You don't have time to learn all you need to know to get your legal house in order and you don't think you have the money to hire a lawyer to do it for you.

Having made that mistake, I want to help you avoid making the same mistake in your business. With advances in technology and systemic efficiencies in my law practice, our office can provide affordable legal advice and assistance for your small business. We do this in a couple of ways.

We offer several **monthly subscription plans** that give you access to unlimited 15-minute phone calls and emails with me, access to our online contract and educational library portal, a discount on all legal fees, and additional member benefits depending on your subscription level. This allows you to schedule a call or send me an email and get advice on an issue before it becomes a bigger problem without the concern of what it's going to cost you at the end of the month. As a monthly subscriber, you've already paid for it. It provides certainty in your budget for legal expenses.

Our subscription plans include registered agent service and corporate deadline monitoring and notification. We assist in drafting the annual documents required to maintain your corporate formalities.

Another way we make access to legal services affordable is by providing most of our business services on a **flat fee**, rather than an hourly basis. You will know the total cost before we start the work. The prices of our business services are listed on our website. This provides certainty in your planning and budgeting and no surprises after the project.

For the most current information about our subscription plans and to learn about our subscription and flat-fee prices, visit our website:

LegalAdvocacyHeadquarters.com

Now that you know the top legal mistakes you can make in your business and how we can help you proactively protect it, I invite you to **take the next step**.

THE NEXT STEP

"Far and away the best prize that life offers is the chance to work hard at work worth doing." **Theodore Roosevelt.**

"The way to get started is to quit talking and begin doing." **Walt Disney.**

Congratulations! You made it to the end of the book and are one step closer to knowing the legal health of your business.

From the information included in this book, you should have a better idea of how you are doing in keeping your business out of legal trouble. If you think about each concept and apply them to your business, you will know what areas need work and which areas are okay. With that knowledge, you can get to work fixing the areas that need help.

But if it all seems a little overwhelming, then please take me up on my free offer to talk to you about the legal health of your business. I will send you a pre-meeting Small Business Legal Assessment to complete that we will go over during our meeting.

Not a Sales Call

This is not a sales call and there is no cost or obligation. As an attorney, I am bound by our rules of professional conduct not to solicit your business. I just want to learn about your business and provide guidance for any areas we identify that need improvement. I want to help you proactively protect your business.

Now Is the Time

Proactive advice on your legal matters is much like the commercial general liability insurance you buy to protect your business against slip and fall claims. If you aren't insured and there is an accident or incident, it is going to cost you more than it would have cost you to pay the monthly premium. Getting regular legal assessments and advice now, before a legal problem arises, will help budget the expense now and minimize costs in the long run which gives you more money to reinvest in the business or to put in your pocket.

How to Schedule the Meeting

To schedule your free 30-minute in-person or Zoom meeting, use the link below. We will send you a link to an online pre-meeting Small Business Legal Assessment to complete before the meeting. Thoughtfully completing the form is crucial to a productive meeting. Once you complete the form, we will send you a link to schedule our meeting. I look forward to learning about you and your small business!

LegalAdvocacyHeadquarters.com/letsmeet

Password: LAHQLetsMeet

ABOUT MARTIN PARSONS

Martin retired from the military after spending four years on active duty in the Marine Corps and twenty-two years, part-time and full-time, in the Illinois Army National Guard. While in the National Guard, Martin served in Iraq from 2005 – 2006 with the 2-130th Infantry Battalion in support of Operation Iraqi Freedom.

During different periods of his National Guard service, Martin owned or operated several small businesses, including the bar and live music venue discussed in the introduction.

After retiring from the military, Martin decided to attend law school and graduated from Southern Illinois University School of Law. After graduation, he practiced business and employment law in Carbondale, Illinois for two years before joining the faculty of SIU School of Law to reestablish its Veterans' Legal Assistance Program.

He left SIU School of Law to focus his time and effort on assisting entrepreneurs proactively protect their small businesses and spend more time with his family.

Martin is fascinated with advances in technology in the legal profession and continually studies ways he can automate processes to provide legal services more efficiently and cost-effectively to small business owners.

RESOURCES

I shared several suggested resources throughout ***The Top 10 Legal Mistakes Entrepreneurs Make In Their Small Businesses***. To make it easier for you to access these resources and for me to update them, I created a single webpage with all those links and resources. There are also several bonus resources included as well. This resource page is only available to readers of this book.

As I find more useful information or resources, I will occasionally update the website. The resources and bonuses can be accessed here:

LegalAdvocacyHeadquarters.com/resources

Password: LAHQResources

NOTES

NOTES

AN EXCLUSIVE INVITATION

Starting and running a small business requires a great idea and a lot of hard work. Creating and marketing your unique product or service takes a lot of time, energy, and focus. With your singular focus on your outstanding product or service, you often neglect some of the necessary legalities of your business.

As a small business owner, I understand those challenges. That is why I help entrepreneurs proactively protect their small businesses through annual reviews of their business operations, affordable access to legal advice and counsel, and advocacy if faced with legal challenges so you can minimize liabilities and maximize your profits.

The first step in knowing the legal health of your business is a thorough review of your business operations. As a reader of this book, I invite you to schedule a free 30 minute in-person, or Zoom, meeting with me to go over our Small Business Legal Assessment. I look forward to learning about your small business!

Schedule your free meeting today at:

LegalAdvocacyHeadquarters.com/letsmeet

Password: LAHQLetsMeet

CPSIA information can be obtained
at www.ICGtesting.com
Printed in the USA
LVHW110346180322
713450LV00012B/110